FOUR PHASES:

Lost, Impermanence, Bittersweet, Caring

DR. IAN PRATTIS

Manor House

Library and Archives Canada Cataloguing in Publication

Title: Four phases: lost, impermanence, bittersweet, caring / Dr. Ian Prattis.

Names: Prattis, J. I., author.

Description: Poems.

Identifiers: Canadiana 20220214646 |

ISBN 9781988058795 (hardcover) |

ISBN 9781988058788 (softcover)

Classification: LCC PS8631.R396 F68 2022 |

DDC C811/.6—dc23

Cover art: *Four Seasons* by artist Carolyn Hill
(www.carolynhill.ca).

First Edition
Cover Design-layout / Interior- layout: Michael Davie
148 pages / 24,000 words.   All rights reserved.
Published 2022   / Copyright 2022
Manor House Publishing Inc.
452 Cottingham Crescent, Ancaster, ON, L9G 3V6
www.manor-house.biz   (905) 648-2193

This project has been made possible [in part] by the Government of Canada. « *Ce projet a été rendu possible [en partie] grâce au gouvernement du Canada.*

Funded by the Government of Canada
Financé par le gouvernement du Canada

WHERE POETRY TAKES YOU...

ACKNOWLEDGEMENTS

My newest book – *FOUR PHASES: Lost, Impermanence, Bittersweet, Caring* – deals with poetry and prose at four different levels that are necessary to balance our world. Severe Climate Change is already upon us and needs swift action to give homo-sapiens a chance of survival. However, the global pandemic and Russia's war devastating Ukraine may detrimentally affect the world from taking the possible route to a live-able Earth as we know it.

I think of my students at Carleton University in Ottawa, and friends meditating at Pine Gate Sangha in my home. I dedicate this book to stand in their light moving forward.

I offer a deep bow of gratitude for the Testimonials for this book. I appreciate the views of each person and am humbled by their trust in my work. My thanks to Jana Begovic for writing the Introduction and Shobha Gallagher for the Foreword. I'm also very appreciative of the testimonials from Claudiu Murgan, Dr. Kimberly Brayman, Susan Taylor Meehan, Derek Blair, Carol Gravelle, Pema Namgyal, Jagjeet Sharma, Professor Koozma J. Tarasoff, Germaine De Peralta and Suha Mardelli. My thanks also to Carolyn Hill for the book cover painting.

Finally, my thanks also to publisher Michael Davie and Manor House for publishing and releasing my book to a world audience.

INTENTION

It is not for me to write poems about Indigenous lore. The Residential Schools in Canada provided a genocide concocted by churches, governments, priests and nuns to eradicate their origins.

I deeply cried and was also enraged at their cruelty, but realized that was not useful. So I created the Dr Ian Prattis Scholarship for Indigenous, Black and Racialized students at Carleton University in Ottawa, Canada. I was a professor at Carleton University from 1970 – 2007 and present the scholarship to graduates that are diligent and intelligent.

With the discovery of the burials of Indigenous children all over Canada I urge readers to please donate to the scholarship to support Indigenous, Black and Racialized students to continue into our mutual future. Contact: https://futurefunder.carleton.ca/giving-fund/dr-ian-prattis-scholarship-for-indigenous-black-and-racialized-students/

I created the scholarship from the revenues of my books. The annual value is $2,000 and is awarded annually by the Dean of Graduate and Postdoctoral Affairs on the recommendation of the chair of the Department of Sociology and Anthropology. This scholarship and my writing brings forward my responsibility of holding the pen as a posture to place words in a sequence that hopefully resonates in the reader's mind.

I have a sense of reciprocity about what I felt was necessary to heal the world from climate emergency and pandemic.

The words play their part throughout as a sort of call and response meter that leans on kinship and community rather than corporate greed. The poems and chapters in this book become as seeds in the mind of the reader, so my work cannot be buried or lost. The emphasis on Indigenous Wisdom pulls chapters together while being aware of how easy it is to fall into destruction.

Introduction:

Prattis' new collage of writing, divided in Four Phases is threaded with the shimmering gold vein of his gentle poetic activism, through which he gathers us in a literary embrace, and nudges us toward a shift of consciousness in our relationship with nature and each other.

His disenchantment with the state of affairs and the ever-increasing violence in the world, and his utter shock and white-hot rage over the discovery of torture and murder of children in residential schools, he alchemizes not only into poetry and inspiring articles, but also into concrete action. One such luminous example of positive action is the establishment of the Dr. Ian Prattis Scholarship for Indigenous, Black and Racialized students at Carleton University in Ottawa, Canada.

Prattis' profound and compassionate reverence for the natural world, reflected as an ever-present leitmotif in his verses, reveals his genuine sense of belonging within the oneness of the Universe, because, as he says, "every molecule engages in the Universal threads," and by damaging and wounding the external world, we inflict harm on ourselves.

His verses,   "Silver birches silhouette the sky,

Sway and breathe

bend and whisper in the canyon…"

pulse in the singing rhythm of all Creation, unveiling Prattis' delight in nature. With a soothing meditative and aesthetic cadence of his verses, as well as his spiritual exaltation over the beauty of nature, Prattis succeeds in enlarging, even if only temporarily his readers' sense of sympathy and compassion for the planet.

Through his poetic eyes, we sense wonder in the birch tree, and glory in the canyon echoing its whispers.

Prattis still writes with excited hope that we may wake up from our slumber of apathy and take action.

Poetry is not his pastime, but a driver of change and with his words, Prattis shakes us gently to the disturbing realities of climate change, injustices, cruelty etc.

His poetry becomes a beacon lighting the path to a less violent future, by inviting us to engage in introspection of our own demons, as well as in exploration of our capacities and potentials to bring more goodness into to the world.

Jana Begovic, Poet, Novelist, Senior Editor of *Ariel Chart Literary Journal*

TESTIMONIALS

Dr. Kimberly Brayman, Licensed Psychologist:

Dr. Ian Prattis's words light the soul and warm the heart; they brought me into sunlit canyons, by banks of racing rivers, and into moments of remembering how precious this world is, and how fragile our place here. As I read, I felt the intergenerational lineage of wisdom, and the need for both steady action and stillness. All of us who care so deeply for this world, and those that don't give the ticking clock of self-destruction much heed. All need to read his words.

Susan Taylor Meehan, Writer:

Ian Prattis has written another brilliant love letter to Planet Earth. Blending poetry and prose in a novel format, he takes us through a series of lyrical odes to the beauty and transcendence of nature, then mourns its loss at the hands of careless and often rapacious human activity. These are familiar themes to us all these days; however, Prattis proposes a new approach, a new mindset, to stop the destruction and rediscover our harmony with the natural environment. Using his own spiritual journey as a guide, he illustrates the power of peace, respect, compassion and courage to first, change ourselves, and then, to join in community to bring these truths to the world. He does not minimize the challenges we face. But he does not give in to despair; this is a book of vision, of compassion and hope, a must-read for all those seeking a new way to live in harmony with ourselves, our fellow humans, and our natural world.

Claudiu Murgan, author of 'Crystal Cloud':

It's been a long time since I read poetry. This genre doesn't cross my path too often and it has to be recommended by a trusted source before I log precious time to read it. In FOUR PHASES: Lost, Impermanence, Bittersweet, Caring, Dr. Prattis has created a sublime eco-system of imagery and feelings that transports the reader to the deepest place of safety, love, and gratitude. The souls that had their physical journey cut short can now find peace as they have been acknowledged through verses that weaved them back into the fabric of nature.

Carol Gravelle, Writer:

Through the words, in the lines, traveling through the paragraphs, the images, the authentic embrace of nature's passion through her coarse river currents, colorful tree canopy, symbols of place in Nature as she is found in us soars in the poems such as "Creation Calling" and "The River Speaks" while the circle of Life and Death speaks of the sweeping power of water and her finger to mold and unmold any tree caught on the rocks' edge as depicted in "Ancient Tree in Winter." Dr. Prattis illumines the path and calls us to listen to the millennial old song of Nature's hidden beauty.

Derek Blair, PhD:

Like many people, I often find myself lost in work and life. Ian Prattis' FOUR PHASES is an escape from the rational and chaotic world that some of us find ourselves caught in. The author has a unique way of telling his story through verse – but also inviting readers to create their own. My favorite example of this is "PHASE FOUR: Caring for the Planet." Here, Prattis assembles symbols and metaphors - such as rivers, seasons, oaks, children, and the muse - to convey an important message about the planet and the environment. This is a message that we can't hear too often. At the same type, these same symbols and metaphors hold deep messages about being human. The Muse, our inner creative voice, encourages us not to forget the creative, spontaneous, more eternal version of ourselves. Autumn encourages us to be mindful of what's really important to preserving and maintaining ourselves. The Oak encourages us to be strong and find ways to be resilient in life. The author cleverly uses symbols to make the connection between our own health and the health of the planet. This is a book for everyone. But especially for people who need a meaningful escape from the hectic rush of life. Readers will find themselves swept away by the eternal metaphors and messages in this book. This is a great read.

Pema Namgyal, Tibetan Poet:

Dr. Prattis' new book "FOUR PHASES: Lost, Impermanence, Bittersweet, Caring" helped me to see our current state of the world through poetry and prose. We live in a dire need of better understanding and a different way of living. Through the author's deep connections with many spiritual traditions he showed me, not only that we have the knowledge and means, but also that we can live ecologically in a sustainable way. This coincides with Tibetan poetry.

Jagjeet Sharma, author/poet/OIW Board member:

Award winning author Dr Ian Prattis once again has created a masterful piece. Each poem is carefully crafted with an abundance of metaphors. The old oak tree evokes the usefulness of *the gnarled Oak tree*; they are old but they are useful especially for *children to climb* and they *set a course for ocean adventures.* Dr Prattis makes us travel with him into nature with his poem *creation calling*, and rivers in *River speaks* and the people of the camp. He takes us on a journey where Mother Earth speaks and we listen.

He makes us see and breathe in nature; the season of Autumn, we can visualize the colors and the beauty in his beautifully woven words. Dancing of the eyes he unfolds nature and wants us to see the beauty as it unfolds. The collection is captivating and breathtaking.

Professor Koozma J. Tarasoff:

This book raises the fundamental issues of peace, climate change, Coronavirus pandemic, respect for nature, and the survival of our species deserves public attention. Ian Prattis, retired anthropology professor in Canada's capital Ottawa, Guru in India, Zen teacher, Founder of Friends of Peace, and award winning author attempts just that. He does it by combining nonfiction with poetry (an innovation in itself), shows us how to set a moral example to our children, uses metaphors of kindness to make good things happen spontaneously, and gives us the tools of dealing with stress and burnout. All this was done by a mature man who once befriended a wolf as a pet, met with female shamans, and went to India for two years of training with wisdom people. With a gentle smile, he invites us to walk carefully as we breathe in and out in search of peace, healing and mental health. On our part, we need to visualize a better state of being by connecting reality to the magic state of mind and the silence within. This path is courageous, but requires us to pay attention to our surrounding ecology. In search of peace, for example, we need to get to know the stranger if we are to survive on our beautiful planet. Bravo, Ian, you have given us hope in a troubled world. For the purist at heart, Ian offers the following: 'Activism without mindfulness practice can lead to disillusionment. Also, spirituality without an engaged expression is equally unbalanced.'

Germaine De Peralta, Journalist and Reiki Master:

Dr. Ian Prattis' poems speak of nature's birth, death, and rebirth as she engages with man through time. His poetry weaves in and out of our senses like a bouquet of classical music symphonies that sing of nature's innocence and purity, her generosity and unconditional love. Yet these rhapsodies are spliced with stark and unforgiving images of nature's imminent destruction as a result of man's neglect and egocentric ways. The poems may eat away at one's conscience. They sometimes scold us, then instruct us. They lament those who honored nature. Then gently lead us to a space of silence, peace, and awareness. The last section of Ian's book, "Caring," is nature reborn, noticed, nurtured. Her unconditional love is reciprocated by us. As a result, she is resurrected in all her beauty, sensuality, spirituality, and joy. This book is a masterpiece.

Suha Mardelli, Ottawa Independent Writers, Board Director:

The poems and articles are wonderful. Ian brings three-dimensional form to Nature's words, layering wisdom in between the respect and mindfulness he has acquired through his journey towards self-actualization. I found myself being carried to the edge of a cliff and ruefully watching how we treat this beautiful planet: not good in fact, but we knew this already. Through the poems, I heard every creature's pain, and celebrated the people doing good in our stead. Ian eulogizes about Gord Downie with such eloquence that even a New Canadian or a non-Canadian will appreciate the impact of our foremost lyrical activist. "The Forest" is a beautiful poem about something so many of us do every day— go for a walk. This walk through the woods is sad because Ian has cleverly placed it in Phase 2: Impermanence, reminding us with subtle elegance that Man has made it so our surroundings will not outlive us, like they were meant to. Man's arrogance is infuriating and humiliating. It sends a strong message that the complicated solutions Man has tangled up in to save the planet are unnecessary distractions. The real solution is far more simple - very profound. Whoever reads Ian's new book will go out and hug a tree. Thus, there is hope for our salvation.

Four Phases / Dr. Ian Prattis

FOREWORD

The Time for Wakefulness

This is a deep journey through the heart of nature, her elements, the earth, ancient wisdom, the threads of the universe that are woven into our cells.

Ian Prattis' new book ***FOUR PHASES: Lost, Impermanence, Bittersweet, Caring,*** explores planetary and environmental issues we have ignored, abused and disconnected with. It may be a soft voice in most parts, but it is incisive, a "scalpel of poetic musings" that probes the consequences of our actions towards nature, the planet, the responsibility of the legacy we are leaving behind for the next generations.

This award-winning author has woven a montage of shining poetry, poignant essays, epiphanies, short pithy stories, multi-dimensional shamanic journeys, deep Indigenous wisdom, the Buddha's path of mindfulness, the Hindu lessons of surrender-fullness and our lost connection with family and generations.

The bevy of literary expressions emerges as one crystal voice from a deep chamber. A voice that breaches the surface to make us seriously ponder what we have ignored, shunned, or run away from.

The author states that he bravely goes into literary work. "A stone tossed into the oceans of life" - as he terms it. For me, I see it as a shimmering river that flows into a collective soul-scape. We can hear and feel the scrunch of our feet as we walk through those forests, marvel at the fresh rhapsody and scent of spring shoots, the flaming russets and gold sheens of autumn.

But, we also sense "the quietness of dark pines" that look down from high and "say very little…the echoes we cannot hear." And yes, we "no longer speak of seasons or note the flight of geese…we ignore the language of the whales calling…"

While creating that metaphorical clearing in the woods or sky or ocean, the author also stokes that much needed long pause. Here in that space of is-ness, we face our inner demons, anchor the wisdom of the Elders, yoke in the urgent importance for the younger generation to understand "the meaning of rivers, forests and mountains."

This is the time when spirituality needs to be balanced with engaged expression, Prattis notes in his essay, "Burn Out, Take Refuge."

At the same time, activism needs to embrace the spirit of mindfulness … to spring from that space of stillness.

In these times of Covid pandemic, Prattis talks about the wisdom of walking meditation, where our footstep and conscious breathing becomes the "brilliant piece of engineering to quiet the mind and body."

How often we forget these profoundly simple truths in the busyness and buzzing haste of our lives. To seek refuge and strength in that togetherness of the community of spiritual practice.

In his poem, The Forest, there is this single aspen tree, "lonely, waiting for companionship, fragile in its aloneness, in our aloneness." He stands within her circle. "And for a brief moment neither were alone."

Beneath the dermis of Prattis' writings there breathes the soul of engaged spiritual activism, of a deep care for nature conservation, ancient Indigenous wisdom, the hauntingly real Shamanic journeys, and more importantly the need to reconnect, nurture and nourish mother Earth.

~ Shobha Gallagher, Freelance Writer

TABLE OF CONTENTS

PHASE TWO: IMPERMANENCE

PHASE THREE: BITTERSWEET

PHASE FOUR: CARING FOR THE PLANET

Four Phases / Dr. Ian Prattis

PHASE ONE: LOST NATURE

Four Phases / Dr. Ian Prattis

1.   Nature Ignored

The treads of boots
leave prints in the snow,

banked softly in the quietness

of dark pines.

Looking down from high
the trees say very little.
Resting through winter,
memories in whispered moments
waiting for the Spring sap surge.

The jagged boulder
in the middle of the path,
another kill-site for Winter.
Easily upends us,
bringing death everywhere
to the figment at the void.

Silence dominates broken feathers.

From blood in snow.

The echo we cannot hear.

No memory weaves our mind,

static speaking over media chatter.

Too busy counting those lost in pandemic

while greenhouse gas infiltrates our lungs.

Thus, we are broken.

No voice beyond the senselessness

of this COVID death.

Just burning bodies in the frigid dark

ripping open without a chance,

while fireflies point stars

without knowing their names.

No longer do we speak of seasons

or notice the flight of geese.

There is only death

frozen in the forest.

Without sense of the loss

we blindly suffer

and decline to roam and rattle in lost realms.

Locked down sterile humans,

unable to procreate,

have now become our myth.

Everything else

stretches our lives, draws the veils

articulating crazy shifts.

Poetry takes us deeper if only we know how.

Trees, rivers, rocks, seas and mountains

survive in our absence.

Oceans are lost to our minds,

as we ignore

the language of whales calling.

- unable to hear their symphony,

or see spring blossoms cast a rainbow

in summer rain.

Boot prints in the snow

are all we leave behind.

2.   Too Late For Refuge

We seek refuge

but can find no place

that waits for flames to inflame logs.

Nothing to keep us warm,

despite dreams stuffed in torn pockets

where our stolen names are never known.

We leave our breath

to play in broken sanctuary.

Our hidden oxygen is not used

at the same time.

A young woman transpires

to make her way, too stubborn to die

behind barricades of fire.

She wore a blue summer frock

without shoes,

dancing across the road,

reflected in the window

of the baker's shop.

Departing with two baguettes,

she returns to sanctuary

to breathe and survive, she dares to

clutch the dandelion parachutes descending.

As baguettes morph into space

crushed by burdens,

life pauses through tired surrender.

Retracing empty footsteps

through years of harrows,

looking for red wine

only to find the taste of blood.

Worlds bigger than ours

tower over with huge anger,

yet hold a delicate fragility.

They dwarf homo-sapiens

left behind by stupidity.

Humanity without knowledge

is why trees cried

over the travesty of barren oil sands

and coal mines.

Trees have a different music -

a sophisticated internet that

creates majestic forests and fires

- they are the epiphany of inter-connection.

Cedar forests

hold what is natural,

Without pain and desperation

to soothe hurts beyond danger

all required by Mother Earth.

A new tapestry rebounds

and evolves to welcome

the rising up of mountains,

forests, oceans and the return

of water creatures.

It masters the unthinkable haunted decline.

All intensely watch humanity,

which only consumes more.

Desperately the Cedar forest

reaches out to homo-sapiens,

who cannot see

that animals leave their tracks in the mind.

3.   Moving Dreams of Nightmares

Dreams smooth then haunt

out of mind's reach.

The time between sleep and waking

throughout our bones.

Huddled in dark clusters,

we speak for the dead

feeding off our ragged moments of fears

and sorrows from long time ago.

Then we were

haunted, seeking our better selves

in the desert tumbleweed

where the worst of our actions dominate.

Sharing universal shards of memory

breaking through greed and racism,

screaming that our world

is now different.

Black Lives Matter

along with all lives -

remind us that we are better

than vague clusters of nightmares.

Clearing moments of mind

desperately rise to find

that step beyond despair.

In a language of sighs and nods

to be perfectly understood,

the balmy evening hides moonlit stars,

shimmering through tall pines

from across the river.

His hands shake like tall grass

bending in the squall of rain.

Thinking her fingertips

were placed on the grave

of his loved one.

She hears every soft word

he murmurs.

4. Ecology Matters

The endpoint of patriarchal culture

sours and scorches our planet

with murderous wars and dirty destruction.

Where is the ecological force

yours and mine,

to create strength and balance

in words of action?

Our scathing scorn about billionaire greed

awakes realization

that their doomed progeny

is nothing but broken shards.

These well-written words

in new horizons and literacy

become the environmental charge

to bring strength to the center.

Yet fear pulls the autumn sky down

to force us mute,

streaked by shattered hailstorms

ripping clouds beyond the mind.

Desperation manipulates wealth for moguls

as the sinking sun

dissolves the moon's glance

to sparkling stars in life's endurance.

I grasp time to pass by the stench

of vulnerability,

and bring power to fill the way guides us

to ensure that Ecology Matters.

5.   Death of Orca

The oceans, strangled by plastic

intrude upon Orca's passage.

Where her pod chokes deathly garbage

starving her sacred calf.

The moon fails to help Orca,

screaming at her worst dreams.

The waiting desolation turns dark

prompted by empty humans

not realizing they are killing

a sister, brother, mother with plastic discarded.

Our garbage,

gathers in bays and oceans fills bellies,

bringing sure death to Orca.

Sister Orca does not understand

their betrayal.

When her calf drops with eyes closed

to the bottom of the sea,

we are guilty

as mere shapeshifters without compassion

only mandated for death.

Ancestors beyond our present reach

seek out extinction and silence

- a shrug their only remaining echo.

Can I keep Orca alive

and sustain her complicated Pod?

Listening to the sea from my house

on the cliffs over the sea,

yearning for glimpse and sound

from white and black.

She does not need human garbage

…… and neither do I.

Humanity is so screwed up!!

6.   Colonial Man

Multi-yellow corn emerges

from summer's raised beds,

heavily harvested,

as gentle showers drop

water over rosemary leaves.

Autumn rains

wash the flagstones,

preparing winter snow

to cling beneath cedar boughs.

Preparing Christmas feasts

from the time of spring seeding,

sweat of summer,

and careful bounty of harvesting.

All shared with season's conversations,

despite Colonial Man planting his crops

with deadly pesticides

that burn the Earth.

Indigenous knowledge of plants

and knowing humans

defy Colonial Man's steps.

They take care of childhood futures

with agreements between humans, earth,

creatures, water and fine air.

The cultivations by Colonial Man

are footsteps that lead to extinction.

Reciprocation destroyed ..

…. nothing left

for human evolution.

7.   Disused Mill at Chaudiere Falls

The raging falls at Chaudiere slip away,

as muscles strain and gasp

thrusting canoe blades deeper

against the rip of piercing eddies.

Inch by inch the boiling current

forces the cedar canoe into a backwater

where the might of industry lay dead.

The pulp mill, disused and silent,

still magnificent in decay.

A new beauty filters through its broken arches

while offering industrial neglect.

Now an eyrie for pigeons,

dead trees, arch and rubble

define the river's cascade over rills of rock.

The old mill's disgorge insists forcefully,

its grip carries the cedar downstream,

past the sculpture of decaying industry.

A disused mill, now dead,

provides that burst of mortality

that knows nature's ultimate insistence.

8.   Torched

She recognized the lengthy gait of the man walking toward her on the beach.   "Simon, what are you doing?" she exclaimed.

He snapped round, trying to hide the petrol can in his hand. Sweat beaded on his face and stained the armpits of his shirt. He muttered a curse and shouted angrily, "It's none of your damn business. Get away from me." His face twisted with anger. She pointed to the petrol can.

He trembled, all six feet of him, in fear of the determined young woman who had caught him. His jeans and work boots had splashes of petrol on them and his dark eyes searched desperately around to see if anyone else had seen him. "I have to set the house up there ablaze. The owner has not paid his dues to the land owner." Then with a touch of shame, "It's my job to do this. There is nothing else for me in this god forsaken place."

"You will not torch the old man's house."

Simon breathed heavily several times before replying, "If I do not, you know that it will be me that gets torched. That's how it works."

The silence was vibrant with anger, fear and shame. At last she spoke, "How far you have fallen, Simon. You need help."

He stepped forward, desperate to remember better times and snarled at her, "How can you help me then?"

She took the petrol can from his hand and calmly spoke, "The old man has been moved to an institution in the city and will not return."

He then gasped as he saw her unscrew the can and splash the petrol over the wooden door and windows of the small house. She struck a match and threw it on the petrol soaked door.

As she passed the empty petrol can to her eldest brother, the blaze lit the somber evening on the beach. She relaxed and said to him, "Your task is completed and nobody died. It is time you left this place for good."

Simon grimly nodded his head. "I think you are correct."

9.   The Future of War

I want to talk to you about our children and the kind of future we create for them. Do we teach them peace? Or through neglect do we allow violence to flood their minds, hearts and consciousness so they learn war? Even worse, do they live out our own personal wars expressed through our violent attitudes, speech and actions towards them? Are we creating intergenerational violence and trauma?

I ask every adult, particularly men, to deal with their internal wars so that only the best is passed on to our children, not the worst in terms of violence. How do we deal with our internal wars, hatreds and fears?

We must stop running; stop hiding behind our addictions and busyness. We come to a stop, look deeply into the eyes of our children and make a commitment to face our internal demons and transform them by stepping onto the path of compassion. Not by transmitting our wars and internal afflictions to the children of the world. We need community to support us in sacred ceremony, love for ecology, meditation and creative spirituality.

We raise our consciousness by retraining our minds, through refining our speech, attitudes and actions. We show our children the way to peace by learning to be peace. The present level of hate and violence globally has increased dramatically.

Excessive violence has been used to damage our planet and populations. This is not the way to proceed. There is no "them" and "us." We either learn to live peacefully together or we all suffer and die together.

All violence is injustice and we have to teach our children the truth about war. Not about winners and losers, but about the long term suffering on both sides. It is only citizens of the world standing together for peace and saying "No to War; No to Destructive Climate" that will stop it. But the hatred grows and the suffering increases. What can we do as individuals to change this? We go to work on ourselves. First of all we must uproot the violence and war within our minds. To prevent war we nurture non-violence. We practice meditation and prayer for our planet in daily life to transform the poisons within our minds and within our nation.

We enter into true peace negotiations by learning the methods of deep listening, of respectful and non-violent communication; by understanding and bringing our mindless, selfish agendas to a stop. We create peace by knowing that compassion is the antidote to violence and hatred. We must also make peace with Mother Earth. If we injure Mother Earth with deadly poisons, we injure ourselves. Our civilization has caused such deep harm to the earth that we humans may soon become an endangered species.

The solution is not political or economic, these are secondary. The primary solution rests on an understanding of robust ecosystems. Every faith and spiritual tradition must renew its ethics and responsibilities and honour the interconnected nature of humanity with Mother Earth. We must make it clear to our political and corporate leaders that the violence they commit in our name is no longer acceptable. We must hold them to account and influence them with our clarity, wisdom and courage. The actions we take now are shaping the possibilities for future generations.

Many years ago, (2008), I published *Failsafe: Saving the Earth from Ourselves*. I wrote about homo sapiens as perhaps a failed genetic experiment. I delivered the content of this book to students at Ottawa's Carleton University in a television course I created on "Ecology and Culture." Halfway through the course I looked out at the young, eager students and offered an apology – that my generation had not left a healthy planet for them. Much later in 2019, I participated in the climate strikes on Parliament Hill in Ottawa. I recalled my apology when surrounded by thousands of magnificent children. It was quite emotional for me to hear them shouting out for politicians to get behind the science. I was in admiration of their strike, yet sad that earth matters had not changed for the better. I noticed that I was not the only grandparent who cried a bit.

However, a brilliant pushback to climate denial had been made by Polly Higgins, a fellow Scot. She was a barrister and created a world-wide campaign to criminalize *ecocide*; the name given to describe the destruction of ecosystems by the carbon cabal and their political lackeys. The legal instrument of ecocide has been promoted by President Macron of France and the European Union. Polly Higgins' idea has garnered worldwide momentum to hold corporate executives and governments liable for the damage they do to ecosystems and humanity. The legal work demanded specific legal changes to protect the earth for future generations of all species.

Unfortunately, Polly Higgins died from cancer on Easter Day, April 21, 2019. Her strong belief was that such a law would change the world. Her work continues with a vast legal team in many countries. Her everlasting quip will never be forgotten:

"I have a choice to protect our Earth, or let it be destroyed."

These are the stakes we all face. International jurist and human rights expert, Valerie Cabanes, has this to say,

> *"The current climate and ecological disruptions are fuelling injustice and geopolitical tensions while those ransacking the planet go unpunished. It is therefore urgent to demand new forms of responsibility and solidarity, by recognizing a fifth international crime, the "crime of ecocide."*

Did anyone notice that degradation of the Earth's ecology was the catalyst for radical Climate Change? Food crops were destroyed by horrendous heat waves as carbon dioxide and methane poured into the atmosphere. Did no one realize that food riots and world panic trace back to one cause – the economic agenda of corporations? The undercover deal between governments and multi-nationals was invested in political and economic structures that centered on the carbon combustion complex. This collective agenda destabilized world order and endangered the world's populations. Billionaire backers protected their profits, downplayed scientific conclusions, and deliberately dulled the intelligence of the general public. They paid selected scientists to promote the position that the existing evidence on climate change does not support crisis warnings. This is a bought and sold lie! Everyone knew the lack of truth – the US government, corporations, and industrialists – all knew the truth. To keep the bottom line of profits in their favour, they were willing to accept that civilization would be destroyed in the not-so-distant future.

The brilliant indigenous response from Robin Wall Kimmerer's *Braiding Sweetgrass: Indigenous Wisdom, Scientific Knowledge and the Teachings of Plants* (2020), is very clear.

> *"What was needed was the wisdom of environmental science, the clarity of philosophical analysis and the creative power of the written word, to find new ways to understand and reimagine our relation to the natural world (283). We seem to be living in an era of economics of fabricated demand and compulsive overconsumption....we continue to embrace economic systems that prescribe infinite growth on a finite planet.....we need reforms that would ground economics in ecological principles and the constraints of thermodynamics (300). Climate change will unequivocally defeat economics that are based on constant taking without giving in return (363)."*

Her views were ignored, yet her sharp, pungent views directed many Canadians to shiver in fear. The summer of 2021 in British Columbia was ridden by mass forest fires, followed by winter flooding that destroyed thousands of farm animals. This massive flooding destroyed roads and railways crippled by landslides across the interior of the province. In the December of 2021 monstrous tornadoes tore through six states in America with over 100 deaths and massive destruction. Such disasters can now be expected every year as a merciless Climate Change rests on the ignorance by homo-sapiens. Yet kindness and open-ness by Canadians and Americans elsewhere brought support to those evacuated from fire, floods and tornadoes. But can they do this every year?

So here is our challenge. We have to experience peace, a deep peace shared between many traditions, cultures and religions. This experience evaporates into nothing if we do not translate it into action. Begin the work on yourselves today, so that your attitudes, speech and actions become an example to your children, friends and communities. Take the practical steps to make peace with Mother Earth in terms of what you consume and support. Then represent your community, in coalition with other communities, to political and corporate leaders. Show clearly that we are choosing peace and harmony within ourselves, within our communities and with Mother Earth.

Together we can do it.

We are Ambassadors of Peace after all.

10.   White Eagle Woman

It was during a gathering of elders in 1978 that I first met White Eagle Woman. She saw how troubled, dense and unaware I was. She enabled my disjointed education and experience with the Indigenous domain of mysticism to evolve into a seamless pattern, rather than remain as random knots stretching across an abyss.

White Eagle Woman was a heavy-set woman with a round face and long black hair, but it was her presence that got my full attention. She rarely smiled, but when she did it illuminated the entire room as her dark eyes lit up with mirth. I was very fortunate to be in her hands. She provided me with shamanic training and teachings over the next three decades. This allowed the mosaic of the past to start revealing itself.

Shamans and medicine people from the Amazon would come to see her. She was a holder of the Midewiwin lineage, a secret tradition of medicine people which stretched across the Americas. At that first encounter at an elder's gathering she told me to attend a Vision Quest on her reserve in Sault Ste, as she had received instructions from her ancestors to train me. That was enough for my attendance.

The eight-day Vision Quest began and finished with a sweat lodge. In between were six days of fasting, prayer and ceremony in the wilderness. White Eagle Woman located me in a small grove of birch and oak trees and I had to stay within a strictly designated area. I found level ground for my tarp and strung it over a frame, built from what I could find within the grove. I placed my four ribbons – yellow, black, white, red - at each of the four directions. The ribbons had meanings for the Vision Quest. One of the oak trees became the symbolic stem of my pipe. The bowl of the pipe was a clamshell with tobacco in it. As the sun moved the tree's shadow, I had to be alert and move the clamshell in the same direction around the base of the tree.

I was very still and silent, observing my territory's nuances, the leaves, smells, insects and rain. White Eagle Woman located herself in a trailer close by and indicated that a medicine bear would visit one of us and to report that to her. Time passed in a seamless flow before we gathered for the final sweat lodge.

On coming off the land, a surprise awaited. I had to consume a half-cup of blueberries and then drink vast quantities of a foul-tasting concoction. This was a cleansing medicine to make me throw up the blueberries. It was quite disgusting. It took a long time before I vomited up the blueberries. White Eagle Woman's comment to me was terse:

"Hmmm - you're holding on tight to resist the truth you need to know!"

White Eagle Woman asked about the medicine bear. Nobody reported experiencing it. In exasperation she turned to me and announced that she had seen the medicine bear visit me twice. What did I remember? I recalled dreaming about a tall, gangly and somewhat goofy creature that was not a bear to my mind. White Eagle Woman immediately threw tobacco on the fire to absolve my ignorant gaffe and instructed me that a medicine bear can take on many forms. The goofy creature was the most receptive one for an idiot like me.

White Eagle Woman chastised my lack of insight while we were all in the sweat lodge. Later on, in private, she quietly revealed the door that had been opened wide due to the medicine bear experience. The visit was to assess whether I was capable of receiving medicine gifts from the past – clarity of seeing and connecting to other dimensions.

White Eagle Woman also identified the female entity that was trying to come to me, as a medicine woman from the American southwest, before white settlement. She even named her: Trailing Sky Six Feathers. She then taught me how to place in my mind the sacred medicine wheel with particular focus on the central circle. That was the location through which Trailing Sky and I could communicate. Furthermore, I was to immediately use the mental medicine wheel to talk to her. I did so, as instructed.

On a daily basis I followed White Eagle Woman's instructions. I would look deeply and dialog with this feminine seed of knowledge in my consciousness. I listened in the silence to Trailing Sky's feminine wisdom to address issues and questions. This became my fieldwork of life, observation and new understanding of consciousness through the eyes of the internal feminine. Silence and skillful deep looking were certainly important, yet I knew that dialog with Trailing Sky was the key. I made diary entries with my questions and misgivings then waited quietly for a reply from within. I wrote with respect and anticipated counsel to arise from inside. It was frequently not what I expected, hence my faith in its integrity.

Shortly after she had taught me how to create a mental medicine wheel, White Eagle Woman asked me to work with her in an intense series of journeying. This was a process of guiding me while in an altered state of consciousness. I was surprised by the invitation. She also ensured that I trained with other shamans in journeying, so I could eventually create a form that would be acceptable for non-indigenous people.

With her, the final journey of five sessions cleared the dross and fears I still carried from my lived-in life. At the same time, it brought the significance of Trailing Sky through to me.

Remembering

Deep breaths rattle in and out of my chest. My legs are shaking, sweat pours down my face and body, eyes are stinging but I can't wipe the sweat away. If I do I'll lose my balance. I keep my arms extended and close my eyes. I stand there, suspended in time and space, my breathing calms. My legs and arms stop trembling and the sweat is no longer coursing down my body.

I open my eyes. Several shafts of light penetrate the darkness. I am standing on one strand of a giant spider web stretching across an abyss, from one side of the cavern to the other. This strand is my sole source of support – a gift from Grandmother Spider. I feel the fibers of the strand beneath each foot as they cradle and balance my slow progress. Eternity seems to pass as I inch along, until finally my left foot comes down on solid rock.

My heart pounds as I look behind for a fleeting, dreadful moment. I peer into the deep, dark abyss plunging below the hard rock platform I now stand on. The grip of the fibers still pulse through my feet as I stand on firm earth. I breathe deeply to steady my nerves and without hesitation walk along the rocky incline leading away from the abyss. Ghouls, creatures and phantoms of all kinds move through the cavern but I walk with determination away from the danger that had entrapped me.

The shock of sunlight blinds me for a moment then I see a verdant valley stretching ahead. The trail leads to a river where I take off my clothes and submerge myself in the crisp, cold water. The danger I carried from the abyss washes away.

I warm myself on a rock and then dress. There is a pair of shoes in my leather satchel. I slip them on and follow the river in the direction of the sun.

A fire flickers beside the flat rock in the centre of a clearing and there is a woman tending it. She is beautiful, tall with long black hair loosely braided on either side of her oval face.

In her buckskin garment she moves as gracefully as a deer. She stops putting wood on the fire and stands tall, watching me. Her dark eyes gravely observe my progress to the center of the clearing where I stand in front of her.

I knew instantly that she was Trailing Sky Six Feathers. She spoke, "We have been expecting you, though wondered if you would get through the dangers of the abyss. The Ancient Shaman of the West is waiting to talk to you. Take the path ahead of you and follow it to the mountain."

The path leads toward the mountains. I feel transported to a valley where there is a small cedar building ahead. The heavy wooden front door is wide open and as I enter, a deep melodious voice greets me. "Welcome, it is about time that we met."

Oil lamps cast a glow over simple wooden furnishings with animal skins thrown over them. There is a central fire and an altar on the east side. I smell the aroma of burning sage and feel the intense sacred nature of this abode.

In front of me is a magnificent old man dressed in a splendid embroidered buckskin tunic and trousers. His hair is white, as is his trimmed moustache and beard. His dark skin makes his smile all the more dazzling. He is easily six feet tall with an athletic body underneath the bearskin robe thrown over one shoulder. All of this vitality seems at odds with his obviously advancing years. His dark eyes penetrate every aspect of my being as he regards me for a long moment. "Come sit with me. We will share some tea."

I make myself comfortable on a bench by the fireplace, feeling at peace as we sip tea together in silence. "There is someone who wishes to meet with you. She passed on to the other side many years ago. Yet she still carries a great burden of sorrow. And that sorrow has to do with you. Are you prepared to meet your favorite Aunt?"

"You mean my Aunt Ruby?"

He nods and there is my Aunt Ruby sitting opposite me on another bench. She is just as I remember her, wearing a fashionable pantsuit, her greying hair pulled back in a bun to display the beauty of her cheekbones and elegant face. When I was seriously ill as a young teen, she took care of me and nursed me back to health. I suffered from a general malaise that my family's doctor diagnosed as rheumatic fever – but it was not that at all.

Had I been born into a society steeped in shamanism, the elders would have seen that this was a shamanic illness, announcing that I was ready for training. But I was not born into such an alert society, and so my shamanic training was postponed until my middle years. But she looked troubled and sad. It hurt to see my aunt so distraught and miserable. Very softly I ask her, "Tell me why you seem so troubled Aunt Ruby?"

"Oh my Ian, there is no *seem* about it. I knew, as did your other aunties, about the sexual abuse you endured at the hands of our second cousin, when he was on leave from the army. We all felt that we had failed to protect you. We took some solace in that you seemed not to remember. So we kept quiet about it, keeping it as a family secret. But I have carried this deep suffering into the grave and beyond, my sisters and your parents too. I am so sorry Ian for not protecting you."

I sit patiently, waiting for her sobbing to subside, and then smiled gently to her. "My dearest Aunt Ruby – please stop your tears. I became aware of the abuse and its effects on me as I got older. In my middle years I had wonderful help from healers and shamans and was able to release the energy of abuse so it no longer harms me as it once did. I even found forgiveness for the man responsible – your second cousin. If I can let go of the suffering, then surely you can do the same."

Her crying stops. "Is this really true Ian?

I replied, "The pain, suffering and violence from the abuse are no longer with me. It is only logical that it is no longer with you. Don't you think so?"

She nods, silent for a while, pre-occupied with her thoughts and suffering. Then she smiles her great broad grin. "You were always my favorite nephew – the little philosopher. I remember our conversations about insects, God and the universe. When you stayed in my home when you were so ill – that was one of the happiest six months of my life."

Her eyes light up. Ruby's sorrow had been lifted and in an instant she is gone.

The Ancient Shaman of the West looks at me with those penetrating dark eyes, "This is what you came to do. It is now time for you to go back."

"Come back Ian." The voice calling to me grows more and more insistent. *"Come back."*

And I travelled back. I was lying down on a bear skin with a pillow under my head. White Eagle Woman, medicine woman of the Ojibwa, sat in her armchair - very carefully observing me on the floor of her home. "I will help you stand up as you will be shaky after that journey. And brush you down with an eagle wing. Then you can sit down on the sofa and tell me every part of your journey. First – drink this glass of water."

I sat down on a brown sofa. White Eagle Woman listened intently as I spoke, occasionally asking me to repeat and clarify the sequence of events I was describing. She was very thoughtful once I finished speaking. I respected her silence.

Then she looked at me shrewdly, as if through new eyes. "This journey had more than I ever expected from you. Grandmother Spider rarely shows herself as a helper. Her job is to spin the threads of the Universe, yet she took time out to build that web across the abyss for you. It is only thanks to her that you could walk out of the darkness of the cavern and begin your intended journey. You were totally unaware of how much her gift means and of the other gifts placed on your journey – and that includes Trailing Sky's appearance at the clearing. She has been brought to your full attention. But what sticks with me the most right now is that you offered gifts to your Aunt Ruby so that her suffering could diminish."

She paused and considered very carefully her next words to me: "The Ancient Shaman of the West is very pleased with your compassion and courage. And so am I."

With that rare acknowledgement I wondered about what else I had missed and still did not understand. This was the state of unknowing from where I began the process of remembering.

PHASE TWO: IMPERMANENCE

Four Phases / Dr. Ian Prattis

11. The Remembrances

This is a meditation on impermanence. Buddha called on his monastics and followers to do this mediation on a daily basis, so that their fears and anxieties are welcomed into consciousness. In this way all other fears may be transformed.

The deep focus on the realities of suffering in the past permits the meditator to touch the Ultimate dimension and take that energy back into everyday life. Waves into Water.

1.	Knowing I will get old, I breathe in.	Getting old
	Knowing I cannot escape old age, I breathe out.	No escape
2.	Knowing I will get sick, I breathe in.	Getting sick
3.	Knowing I cannot escape sickness, I breathe out.	No escape
4.	Knowing I will die, I breathe in.	Dying
	Knowing I cannot escape death, I breathe out.	No escape

5. Knowing that one day I
    will lose all I hold dear today,
    I breathe in,   Losing what I
                                                     hold dear

    Knowing I cannot escape
    Losing all I hold dear today,
    I breathe out.   No escape

6. Knowing that my actions
    are my only belongings,
    I breathe in.   Actions true
                                                     belongings

    Knowing that I cannot escape
    the consequences of my actions,
    I breathe out.   No escape

7. Determined to live my days
    Mindfully in the present moment,
    I breathe in.   Living
                                                     mindfully

    Experiencing the joy and the
    benefit of living mindfully,
    I breathe out.   Experiencing
                                                     joy

8. Offering joy and love each
    day to my loved ones,
    I breathe in.   Offering love

    Easing the pain and suffering of
    My loved ones, I breathe out.   Easing
                                                     suffering

12. The Ascetic at Bodh Gaya

My wish is to record Living Dharma – people, life and experience in both their vibrant and mundanity. I am not so interested in monuments and old bricks, being more in tune with the 14th Dalai Lama:

> *"This is my simple religion. There is no need for temples, no need for complicated philosophy. Our own brain, our own heart is our temple. The philosophy is loving kindness."*

Water walking pilgrims
trace Gautama's searching footsteps.
Threads of centuries of quiet walking
through sand, mud and fields
- mere strands of Mother India,
Footsteps shared happily between pilgrims.

Deep silent journey
to emaciated Gautama's cave
yet to receive succour
from Sujata's grace.

Then with awakening stirring
at Bodh Gaya,
Gautama became Buddha,
asceticism abandoned
for the Middle Way.

No shipwrecked words
followed his compass.
The Buddha's insight brought all pilgrims
to be seekers of Truth.

A morning meditation,
bamboo grove calling,
our hearts wide open.

Bodhicitta dancing with
graceful sweepers of fallen leaves,
behind a plough of words.
Heart wide open
with no horizon or meter.

Cascading into passages that hover,
tracing cosmic runes
at the edge of wisdom.

Words drift by in the morning mist.
A whisper of wind
finds every thought one breathes,
waiting wondrous so long
for cracks in façade's order to crumble.

13. The Buddha Temple

Om mani padme hum.
The ancient from Tibet,
purple robed,
respectfully seated at one side
of the Buddha's seat of wisdom.
Where dharma poured
as rain on minds of disciples.

Resonating through the ages
I close my eyes.
Listening deeply to voices from before,
full of remembrance,
as existence explodes into being.

Opening my eyes to the smile
in the deep brown eyes
of the Tibetan monk.
With permission, I photograph his devotion.

In that timeless moment,
The camera, me, ancien and the Buddha
have no boundaries.

Om mani padme hum.

14. Cremation Pyres

Black specks of ash,
caught by wind,
deposit mortality of unknown others
upon my shirt.

Each smudge a stark reminder
of my own death.

The mark already out of reach,
from my powdered ashes
when caught by wind.
Upon whose shirt and heart
will they find?

There you are dark friend.
I see your ancestral memory
- a hungry ghost
to distort the awesome presence of
Dharma, Sangha and Buddha.

Too foolish and resistant
to drink from the deepening
well of bodhichitta.
Created by pilgrims throughout time.
Our collective compassion
makes the Buddha nectar even
available to you
– hungry ghost.

This the pilgrim's gift and prayer,
to bring succour and life to
the hungry ghost within us.
Miracles and wonders of Mother India alive.

Stunning, overwhelming vistas
'midst dusty feet, facial grime, filth and death.
Walking with sublime peace, happiness and joy
unravels overgrown nature with lost stones,
aware of recycled slabs.

Footsteps shared between extremes
as strange questions arise.
Is this excrement on my shoe from a cow,
buffalo or human?
Does heaven descend upon the Ganges
through cremation, devotion, filth and ceremony?

Who really cares?

Step into the excrement of life
to find miracles and wonders
there all the time.
Everlasting.

India alive with rich compost
for wonders and miracles to flower.
Waiting patiently within
to awaken each heart.

15.   It Hurts, Gord Downie

Dear World, be advised that Canada is closed tonight.
The collective grief of Canadians spills over
when Gord Downie died.
He fought for a better future.
Right Here!
RIGHT HERE!

Too much grief for a country
that loved Gord Downie
yet understood not his intentions.

NOW THEY KNOW.

He celebrated every particle of Canada,
inviting us to his death,
to see his heart placed
with indigenous brothers and sisters:
    -   a Secret Path and Chanie Wenjack –

He did not offer entertainment,
rather a rebuke to residential schools.
Shaming cruelty imposed on indigenous children,
exposing deep scars on Canada's conscience.

His passing was a scorching flame -
bringing reconciliation to the neglected
and the abused.

His flaming torch will not be doused.
I for one pick up this flame …. will you?

Lakota *Wicapi Omani* honours
the "Man Who Walks Among the Stars"
Gord Downie, artist and poet
has gone
with his legacy to Canada's First People.
Mystical magician of music,
Teacher of the Way.

He forced the Nation to confront
its darkest moments of genocide
to indigenous children.
The need for decolonization
was directly thrust
at popes, churches, prime ministers
and all of US!

16.   About the Remembrances

I met a visiting Rishi in 1995 – a holy man from India who recognized me and insisted I go to India for spiritual training.

I took leave from my Canadian university and spent two years as a yogi, where the spiritual treasures of India were opened to me. I went there to teach and train in Siddha Samadhi Yoga, a system of meditation for adults and children. It was committed to global religious harmony and program participants work to heal and transform deeply rooted schisms in Indian society - through rural development, civic responsibility, and anticorruption programs.

Also required was a marvelous outreach to introduce meditation into schools. colleges, universities, and factories. I was privileged and honored to experience so many treasures of India.

While in India, in November and December of 1996, I became seriously ill. As I observed my body's systems crashing one by one, I knew there was a distinct possibility of death. I was surprised by my calm and lack of panic.

As December drew towards its close, I totally surrendered. I will always remember Saturday, December 21, 1996 as if it were yesterday. On that day, I let go of all attachments to my body and surrendered to a sense of freedom never before experienced.

I was living in a small ashram in the city of Mumbai – reserved for saints and holy men. I did not qualify for either category yet felt their grace at hand. I felt at one with all my spiritual ancestors, their wisdom, love, and gentleness as a tangible presence.

One humorous manifestation of that grace occurred one morning when I woke up and opened my eyes to greet one of my swami mentors. He smiled broadly and helped me to sit up, then surprised me with his words: "We are all so happy Ian that you have decided to die with us in India, if indeed you are to die. And we will be most happy should you live."

To the best of my memory I just smiled and said, "Me too!"

He made me some tea with herbs and beamed love and understanding to me before leaving.

I felt very calm about the impermanence of my bodily existence. My heart opened wide.

While I did the meditations on "Looking Deeply and Healing," I thought about my many mistakes, and chose not to deny them or brush aside the bodily pain in this moment, for I knew that the experiences of joy and freedom that were flooding through me were dissolving both.

I felt very simple, that I was living properly. I was without panic and present with whatever arose. I did not fear death. This lack of fear gave me freedom and strength, and opened a huge door to send love and joy to all.

I felt my true self, peaceful, not pulled in any direction.

Despite all that was going on, I was solidly and timelessly present. I could freely share whatever gifts, skills and energies I had. I finally understood the significance of the Buddha's words about The Five Remembrances.

To be with myself at this time—happy and content in the moment—was all I had, and it was enough. As I practiced this meditation,

I felt that each moment of life was absolutely precious and somehow, I was communicating this to all that I connected to.

Before I slept that night, one last meditation secured me in the refuge of all my spiritual ancestors.

Although the focus was on the Buddha, I felt all my teachers and guides throughout lifetimes gathered together inside and around me, without boundaries, and they stayed while I slept. When I fell asleep, I was content and happy.

The next morning, to my surprise and joy, I woke up! Over the next six months, I slowly recovered my health. Friends in North America who tune in to me very closely had booked airline tickets in December to take me out of India to recover. While I was touched by their love, I said no to their proposal. Whatever the outcome, this particular journey was to be in India.

I had written countless Christmas cards to friends and loved ones all over the world and signed them with "Blessings and Love from Ian." That is what I had wanted to send before my death. Then I lived! And I was even more happy that the cards were sent.

My work in progress took me back to India six years later. My wife Carolyn and I embarked on a pilgrimage with Shantum Seth - In The Footsteps of The Buddha - through North India and Nepal in February 2003.

We journeyed to Rajghir, Bodh Gaya, Varanasi, Sarnath, crossed into Nepal at Lumbini and then to Kushinagar, Vaishali and Sravasti.

I composed insight poems to provide a glimpse of experiences that are too immense to otherwise communicate. My wish was to record Living Dharma - people, life and experience in their vibrant mundanity.

The Footsteps of the Buddha pilgrimage was full of wonder and miracles. It was a journey to the center of being so that everyday life becomes a pilgrimage. Every reality I am engaged with is also a pilgrimage.

17.   Silence - the Yasoja Sutra

Ten days before the rainy season retreat Yosaja and his five hundred monks journeyed to where the Buddha held his three month retreat. They arrived in a boisterous way to greet the monks there with loud greetings and lots of talking.

The Buddha heard this uproar and asked his faithful attendant Ananda, "What is that noise?" Ananda replied that the Venerable Yasoja and his followers had arrived and were greeting the resident monks. The Buddha asked for them to come to him, so he could send them away and dismiss them for their noise.

The five hundred monks and their leader bowed to the Buddha and left the rainy season retreat in Jetta Park.

They walked for many days to the east side of Koshala and arrived at the Vaggamuda River. Once there, they built small huts to begin their own rainy season retreat. Yasoja addressed his followers and told them that the Buddha sent them away out of compassion, so that they would practice deeply. All the monks saw this as true and practiced very seriously to show the Buddha their worth. The majority of them realized levels of enlightenment during their three month retreat. The Buddha's rainy season had also finished and he remarked to Ananda that he could discern the energy of goodness and light emanating from the east. He realized that Yasoja and his five hundred monks had achieved something very deep and sent them an invitation to join him.

They arrived quietly in the evening after many days of silent walking to find the Buddha sitting in silence, in a state of concentration called imperturbability – free and solid. When they saw this, they decided as one body to sit like that with the Buddha and entered the same state of silent imperturbability. Ananda approached the Buddha during the three watches of the night and asked him to address the monks. The Buddha remained silent. After the third reminder he said, "Ananda, you did not know what was going on.....I was sitting in a state of imperturbability and all the monks did the same and were not disturbed by anything at all."

In this deep unshakable silence the communication between the Buddha and Yasoja's five hundred monks was perfect so that a deep transmission of insight, freedom and joy went to them.

18.   Ancient Wisdom

During my career as an anthropologist, I was fortunate to encounter many First Nation story tellers across North America: Dene, Hopi, Ojibwa, Algonquin, Inuit – to mention a few. Their poetic recounting of myths and history had a deep impact on how I thought and wrote. I would say that without poetry, cultures implode. Extraordinary indigenous medicine people enhanced my process of remembering the power of the poetic voice. Through their mentoring, I learned how to reconfigure my understanding of time, place and consciousness. I chose to listen to the sacred feminine voice of Earth Wisdom rather than the multitude of competing voices in my deep unconscious.

I made a radical turn in the 1980's to reconstruct anthropological methodology, as the poetic voice was always required for investigation of the cultural other. I felt that the language of the anthropologist could not represent the raw experience of other cultures - therefore poetry was philosophically essential to the work of anthropology. I saw poetry as an uninterrupted process whereas field notes were not. I suggested to colleagues that the poetry of observation is what anthropologists are supposed to be doing. Anthropologists who commit themselves to poetry in order to say something different about field experience are the tricksters and shamans of the discipline. I have been described as much worse!

The radicalization of the discipline and an evolution into a different kind of anthropology was required. A continuation of this perspective emerged several decades later when I brought out a personal volume of poetry in 2018 – *Painting with Words, Poetry for a New Era.* The poems were split into six parts, each with its own distinctive theme.

The final part is dedicated to Ancient Wisdom where an epic poem awaits the reader's attention. It was written when I accompanied two friends on the first leg of their cross Canada canoe expedition.

My good friend, Keith Crowe, teamed up with me and a yellow canoe. I had never undertaken anything quite like this. This long poem about Ancient Wisdom was written during the canoe trip, under oil skins, during portages, while cooking in the rain and once when standing drenched and half clothed in a Quebec laundromat.

My creation of this poem had a double focus. I wanted to leave a document about Canada's wilderness for my grandchildren, so they could be inspired by Mother Earth. When experience and inspiration sparked, I would shout out to Keith in the stern of the yellow canoe that I had to write.

I would bring out the oil skin envelope stuffed with poems about the journey. I also wanted to weave in the Wisdom of the Elders, to speak about Canadian waterways from the reverence of First Nations, so that my grandchildren would understand the meaning of rivers, forests and mountains.

The words "without poetry, cultures implode" leaves the door open for our species and leaders to change. I choose to complete this story with a moment from the focus on Ancient Wisdom. It pulsates with the rhythm of the river and the spirit of nature of its ancient inhabitants. In this epic poem I criticize human greed and its destructive impulses that result in pollution, contamination and annihilation of the natural world.

I am nostalgic for the ancient ways of the people who had held Mother Earth in sacred regard, so I take readers into the heart of nature's Zen-like serenity, and sheer "thereness." The reader is hurled at the same time onto the path of nature's fury expressed through extreme weather conditions.

In spite of being exposed to the merciless harshness of the elements, the poet – that is me - still smiles because I am a part of this world, just like a tree or a rock.

I see Ancient Wisdom as the tabernacle of our collective memory, and I harvest these ancient energies and weave them into my own history.

In the poetry volume of 2018 I took the reader through the immensities of joy and pain, through the infinite and the mysterious.

I dissect the dissonance of the modern world with the scalpel of poetic musings and describe the interflow between the human soul and the spirit of Earth - paving a quest for spiritual evolution and higher meaning.

I provide a poetic narrative of our basest attributes as a species, our greed and propensity toward a savage violence, as well as our ability to love beyond the telling power of words.

Ancient Wisdom awakens the sense of the infinite within us, surging our hearts with the power of their message.

My poetry aims directly for the heart, speaking to the reader in clear and loud words, sometimes screaming the truth. This restores the possibility of the ancient dialogue between humans and nature.

I take a small portion of the epic in order to talk about The Forest. The connection between humans and nature is illustrated with a solitary tree and a man. In each other's presence, their feelings of aloneness vanish.

The Forest

Whisper of wind through pine needles.
Shimmering aspens and soft poplars of the forest.
Green – spring fresh green,
a relief to the year round darkness of the spruce's
darker timbre and twin pronged sheaths.

The river denies our passage
so we walk through sheltered forests

rather than meet
our death by foolishness.

We wander and find herbs, trilliums white in dense bush,
hiding among the wild strawberries
un-bodied with their
rich red summer promise.
Guardian trees, lichen laced,
protest the spring violets pushing upwards.

In the forest a great many entities
of the earth and sky speak of before
and what is to be.

Clearings sunk into the earth
await further visits.

In the center of one clearing
stood a single tall aspen - lonely.
Waiting for companionship,
fragile in its aloneness,
in her aloneness,
in our aloneness.

I stand within her circle
- this tree and I -
and for a brief moment,
neither were alone.

PHASE THREE: BITTERSWEET

Four Phases / Dr. Ian Prattis

19. Anger Boil

Touch the anger,
bring tears dripping down
your face and fingers.

Balance the scream
that permits your exit.
Step into the fire of nihilism.

The pallor of your body's dark history
wanders beside the tide.
Looking for the place
on the ruined planet
as jaguars growl at the boundary
intended to save you.

Who will rescue you?
What remains of our homesteads
boiled and burned in your anger?

20. Beware of Deity

Listen well everyone,
Deity snarled as she
slithered out
knocking the door to the ground.

Idiots, do you not know I am here?
To revile all of you
with fire, sarcasm and scream.
Slashing puny bodies
with inflicted personal pain
until you realize
the steps for Nirvana's crown.

Instead of crumbling to dust
find the volumes of Verdi's
symphonic echoes,
to sing your way to clasp
the direction of Oracle.

Be lifted by Atlas to the stars,
the throne of my Deity.
Then may you no longer bleed anymore.

21. Lament for a Mariner

The sea is very thin this day
that Archie Ruag has gone
- Master mariner, graceful navigator,
wise teacher of ocean mystery.
No more to grace the ocean's ships
Returned to whence he came.

My sons at eleven years and ten,
children in men's mourning
saw him laid to rest
in my place,
as storms and hail swept the cemetery
and their small frames
grew in maturing
of Archie Ruag's final place.

I sit here in Canada
writing, grieving,
knowing the sea is very thin this day
that Archie Ruag has gone.

I saw him last, pale and weary
with calm before his death.
His spirit surrounded by antiseptic ward,
but not beleaguered.

Archie Ruag knew I was not equal
to his dying.

So he spoke gently to me
of ships
and men at sea.

And moorings
safe to guard our boats
from winter's cruelty.
And so, in this way
did he gently rebuke
my lack of courage
in his dying.
So that I may have strength
in my own time
of death.

This is known
to senses awry with grief's knife.
The tears down my cheeks
on a rain wept street,
a quiet meditation
on the knowing of him.

Yes - I miss him.
An anchor gone from my seasons
of the sea.

The sea is very thin this day
that Archie Ruag has gone.

22. Return to Tulum

As tall reeds move with unison in a jungle pool,
selfie sticks clump in swarms
before the ancient monument of Tulum.
Their plastic smiles consume posterity
where I sat with reverence
– years past.

Vacant minds endure with pasted smiles.
I wonder if sacredness
penetrates unbridled progeny
of entitlement, noise and distraction?

Thirty years since I entered the walled city of Tulum,
sequestered behind ropes and strict security.
The price of graffiti, looting and volley ball.

Even now the ancients could still be heard,
presence emerging with stillness and respect,
though silent to oiled sunbathers.
Whistle blowing security guards chase hooligans
from forbidden coastal bays and ceremonial pyres.
Marching them out of where they cannot be.

Years ago I occupied those similar spaces,
but was bound with reverence.
No security guards to police my silent awe.
My whispered wish registers the Mayan radiance.
The Gods Face All Ways,
beacon of ancient history.

Then later swarms appeared.
Legions carried the banner of language and culture.
Serious, bolder, organized, marching in order
like legionnaires in steps.
Tutored by multilingual guides, interpreters and sages
carrying knowledge of Maya intelligence.
These legions dwarfed all selfies and hooligans.

The Gods Face All Ways
were recognized, not mocked.
Venus, the evening star of the Maya
appeared in the night sky,
as the walled city of Tulum emptied.

The *Halach Uimic* dynasty vibrated
through the five openings
of the walled city of Tulum,
into the ceremonial center,

Then East to the Castillo,
misnamed by Juan de Grijalva in 1518,
this majestic monument, a great palace
stood atop the cliff - crowned by a temple
complete with blood-stained sacrificial stone,
sloping steeply to the Caribbean Sea.

Before brazen tourism and tight security
I sat at this Upper Temple three decades past.
Alert to frightening corner-stones facing west,
emulated masks with mouths wide open,
teeth filed.

I stayed some distance from the sacrificial stone
placed on the cliff edge overlooking the Caribbean Sea
tuning-out the hundreds of passers-by,
and there it was…
a similar stone at the foot of the monument,
the mesmerizing energy from time before.
as I sat quietly upon it,

Before then, I could not put pen to paper.
Now, I can.

23. Spirit Guardian

Our first meeting was outside a cabin in the Mt. Currie area of British Columbia. I saw the timber wolf standing in the shadows of a tall spruce nearby. I observed distinctive white markings on his head, chest and forelegs, which were a startling counterpoint to his reddish-brown fur. He moved silently to gain a different vantage point. I went inside and opened a tin of salmon and placed it in front of the cabin. He stealthily approached and I could see how beautiful a creature he was.

The salmon offering was soon devoured as he retreated to the shadows of the surrounding forest. I opened another tin of salmon. He consumed this offering and disappeared as silently as he had appeared. That evening after I turned in to bed, I heard him come up the steps to the veranda. He was nowhere to be seen in the morning, though there were fresh strands of his reddish fur trapped by knots in the wood.

Each night he lingered outside until one evening I opened the cabin door to see if he wanted to come inside. Without hesitating, he entered and curled up on the floor by the hearth. I let him out early in the morning and did not see him again during my remaining time there. On the next occasion that I took refuge in the mountain cabin, he turned up within ten minutes.

He made it clear that I was to follow him by running to the edge of the clearing then back to the cabin steps - several times. I laced up my boots and grabbed my walking stick. He took me on a tour of his territory - through thickets, over hills and in the forest until we came to a wide mountain stream. He swam across. As I was indecisive, he plunged back into the chilly stream, swam to where I was standing and then led me further downstream to a shallower crossing. I took off my boots, socks and trousers and carried them above my head, entering the icy cold water. He swam vigorously past my slow wading.

Once we were both across, he bounded along the bank and ran circles round me in sheer delight. He seemed thrilled I had crossed the mountain stream with him! This beautiful creature was sprawled on the grass studying me closely. For quite a long time he lay prone on the grass - scrutinizing. Then suddenly he rose and promptly bounded off. I got up and slowly retraced my steps. By nightfall I was back at the cabin. There he was on the veranda!

He had shown me part of his territory. It became clear that he was not part of a pack. It was in his mind to live with me in my home in Gatineau Park Forest in Quebec. His thoughts registered vividly with me once I was home. For several months I had dreams about this beautiful creature living in the forest around my home. Some months later I arranged for my son Iain, who lived in Squamish to pick him up from near the cabin. That became the rendezvous. My son drove there in his pickup truck after collecting the strong crate I had purchased online in Vancouver. He wondered why on earth his dad was going to so much trouble for an animal. The timber wolf was at the Mt. Currie cabin - patiently waiting. The journey to

Vancouver Airport Cargo started with the wolf in the cage resting in the back of the pickup. By the time they arrived at the airport, the wolf was on the front seat sitting next to Iain. He had learned how unusual a creature this wolf was during the overnight stay in his home in Squamish.

I had insisted that he describe the animal on the cargo manifest as a dog, not a timber wolf - a necessary precaution. The magnificent creature quietly settled into the cage before it was placed in the cargo section of the plane. He knew where he was going. My son told me later that he was inexplicably reduced to tears by the departure of a wild animal that had captured his heart. I gave my new friend the highly original name of "Wolfie!" My small hermitage in the Gatineau Forest became his new home. I tried to train him until I realized how totally redundant that was. Wolfie could read my mind and would always respond. His gentleness, patience and above all, his loving heart, were felt by everyone he encountered.

Wolfie was instrumental in getting my soon-to-be wife's attention. A friend was taking ballroom dancing lessons and asked me to accompany her, as her partner was unable to. At the Jack Purcell Centre in Ottawa, an elderly Jamaican gentleman was our instructor. He had all the moves to put us through the paces of ballroom dancing. I noticed an attractive blonde woman always dancing the male part with her female friends – they were co-workers. Her name was Carolyn. I asked if she would like to dance with me. Her wide green eyes and gentle smile said it all. Dancing with her was magic. Not once did I tread on her toes during the intricate passages of the Quick Step and the Fox Trot. At the end of the evening, I asked if she would like to meet my wolf. As soon as those words came out of my mouth, I thought she must think this was the worst pick-up line in the world. She paused, smiled and said, "Yes."

Wolfie played his part beautifully. I rolled down the window of my truck and Carolyn could see his magnificence. I should have called him "Hollywood Joe" instead of the rather lame "Wolfie." He placed one paw on Carolyn's shoulder and gently licked her cheek. Carolyn told me later that she fell in love with the wolf first, then thought that there must be something about the fellow who had him. And so began our wonderful togetherness.

This beautiful animal also rekindled forgotten memories of innocence within me. As a child I blithely assumed that nature walked me when I roamed the forest and rivers, stretching time as I explored nature's domain on my way to school. When I found hurt animals and birds, I knew to find a special place within me that touched these creatures before I could be of any assistance. This was all intuitive. It was the way I was and I assumed at that time that it was the way everyone was.

Several years later I was in Sedona, Arizona and looked up my friend Dawson – a trained medicine man. He was a wisdom holder of many traditions – Ojibwa, Hopi, Lakota and the Native American Church and was a legendary figure in Central Arizona. He had met all kinds of people in his capacity as a guide and teacher. Yet his attention and presence never wavered in its intensity as he welcomed all into his orbit of wisdom and patience. Dawson was a slender, muscular man in his sixties, though he seemed much older. His manner was slow and deliberate, gentle but firm. It was the same with people, animals and the desert. He brought a sense of gentle intensity and intimacy to every relationship. The initial connection from that first field trip and movie experience warmed into a close friendship.

He invited me to his sweat lodge, which had four rounds. He used a different circle of spoken words for the third round - the Red Wolf – as he knew I had my own red timber wolf. My neighbour Lisa was looking after Wolfie at my home in the Gatineau forest while I was in Arizona. During the round of the Red Wolf in Dawson's sweat lodge, I felt Wolfie's presence right next to me, but did not pay too much attention. Later that night Lisa telephoned me with the dreadful news that Wolfie had died. I was devastated. The timing of Wolfie's death in Canada coincided with the timing of the Red Wolf round with Dawson. After putting the phone down I knew I had to talk to Dawson. I put on my jacket, picked up the truck keys and opened my cabin door. Dawson was just pulling up in his car. He got out and strode over to me. In characteristic manner Dawson came straight to the point. "Something strange was going on with you during the Red Wolf round in the sweat lodge."

I gasped and burst into tears, as Dawson put his powerful arms around me for comfort. Through my sobs I told him what had happened. Dawson was gentle but firm.

"You need to do a journey for this one, Ian. Before coming here I took the precaution of asking my fire keeper to prepare the grandfather stones for a sweat lodge at my place. That's where you can journey and find out just what happened. And don't tell me that you don't journey, for I know different. Now get in my car."

On the drive to his home near Cottonwood, I related to Dawson the story of Wolfie and how we met. By the time we arrived at his sweat lodge I was in a suspended state. There was only Dawson, the fire keeper and me. The opening round was for chanting to the animal powers, the second round for our prayers to the Earth Mother, the third was the round of the Red Wolf, though with a difference. Dawson took me through a long session of deep breathing, using drums and chants to aid my entry into an altered state of consciousness. The journey was to visit my red wolf. Dawson guided me by trek and canoe to find a stream deep in the mountains. In the altered state of my mind I paddled for a long time until my arms felt very tired. Then turning a bend in the river I came to a clearing straight ahead. There stood Wolfie with a female spirit guardian behind him. I beached the canoe and knelt before Wolfie, putting my arms round his strong neck while he licked every part of my face. Then I sat beside him as we looked out at the river.

I asked Wolfie, "Can you tell me why you died when you visited me in Dawson's sweat lodge during the Red Wolf round?"

It was the female guardian who replied, "This creature so loved you that when he tuned into energies that could harm you in the third sweat lodge round, he placed his body in their path so you would be spared damage. That is what took his life."

I received this news in silence, placing one hand on Wolfie's strong back. We just sat side by side watching the flow of the river. The female guardian gently spoke again, "It is time for you to return."

I took my leave and did not look back at Wolfie as I could not bear to break down. As I pushed the canoe off the beach into the grip of the river, Wolfie bounded across the clearing and jumped into the canoe as the female guardian said, "He will always be with you in spirit form – protecting you still."

Then the female spirit guardian stepped into the canoe. I did not look back but my heart leapt with joy. I knew that she had sent Wolfie to provide me with protection. I paddled away with deep gratitude and happiness, knowing that the energy of Wolfie and the female guardian surrounded me.

Dawson splashed some water on my face. I came back to present time and space from the shamanic journey. The final round was a thanksgiving round. I was instructed by Dawson to keep Wolfie and the spirit guardian always in my mind and heart.

The journey was over. Dawson smiled and I bowed deeply to him.

24. Burn Out, Take Refuge

Over the years I have observed many young activist friends in the peace and environmental movements becoming overwhelmed and suffering from stress and burn out.

Despite my best efforts, they have not always been open to mindfulness practice. I firmly believe that activism without mindfulness practice will lead to burn out and disillusion of one form or another. I consider spirituality without an engaged expression to be equally unbalanced.

I encourage all of us embarking on this 21st century adventure in Peace and Planetary Care to root ourselves deeply in mindfulness practice on a daily basis.

Touch the stillness of non-action first of all, so that our ensuing actions come from a place of effortless abundance and clarity. This is how we can take care of stress, burnout and disappointment. Guidance is essential. It is there in abundance from Thich Nhat Hanh, as he specifies very clearly how to reach out for help. He encourages us in times of adversity, despair and burnout to take refuge in the sangha – the community of spiritual practice.

Elder brothers and sisters in the community who are steady, patient and wise can help us step out of despair and anger by practicing meditation with us, returning us to mindfulness in order to take care of our distress. Be sure to take refuge in wise and steady friends.

There is no point in taking refuge in folks who are as bummed out as you are! Then there is taking refuge in the dharma – through practices like Deep Relaxation, Touching the Earth, of heeding the Mindfulness Trainings to protect us from making harmful decisions.

There is also taking refuge in the Buddha whose awakened mind is in the sutras that guide us step by step from despair to happiness. Each Refuge encourages us to foster positive and wholesome mental formations rather than fostering further despair and angst. Instead of running away from our fear and distress by hiding it under addictive behaviors, we learn from Taking Refuge just how to embrace and transform our fear and distress – first of all by clearly recognizing it.

We have to become good gardeners of the mind to do this. It takes skill, mindfulness and retraining to become a good organic gardener, so that the garbage in us is turned into rich compost rather than rejected or repressed. It also takes much understanding based on a non-dualistic view – accepting and recognizing just what is there in the mind. So if our mind is dark with sorrow or anger we recognize that this is just so.

With awareness we know how to practice walking meditation to take care of the mind-state recognized. Without the darkness and sorrow we would have no idea about the light dance of happiness.

Instead of being overwhelmed by darkness, which can so easily happen, we use our skills of practice to recognize our mental states, nurture and transform them to a state where there is no danger of being overwhelmed. This non-dualistic way of looking at our mind states makes good sense, particularly as the alternative of suppression, of not practice, of not mindfulness, keeps us caught in the burnout, deeply mired in suffering with the conviction that there is no way out of this misery. This "not" alternative rapidly leads to depression, mental illness and damage to others as well as to ourselves. The mindfulness alternative of developing the necessary skills is a very wise and therapeutic option.

You may see for yourself the value of taking refuge in sangha eyes to guide your perceptions; of taking refuge in the practices, trainings and sutras for guidance in order to apply the energy of mindfulness to the energy of burnout.

With the assistance available through taking refuge in the Three Gems – Buddha, Dharma and Sangha – the practice comes alive as a highly strategic set of tools and skills to produce transformation of the suffering caused by difficult and painful circumstances that lead to burnout.

Activism is full of crises, curve balls and disasters. But even so we do not have to be overwhelmed and crushed by them. Mindfulness practice helps us. Understanding and compassion hone our skills so that we become excellent gardeners of the mind.

25.   The Rishi and Arrisa

There was a Rishi who lived in a remote part of northern India. Many people from the surrounding villages were drawn to this kind and compassionate holy man. They listened to the clarity and love in his talks, which were drawn from the universal wisdom tradition of the Vedas.

His teachings and guidance became part of the fabric of village life and he conducted daily and seasonal prayers, and ceremonies, to honour the earth and sacred traditions he had immersed himself in since childhood. His spacious hermitage was set apart from the villages. It was like the central hub of a great wheel, the congregating point for the surrounding communities.

He was honoured and revered for the gentle manner in which he brought people to their own deep quiet communion with God.

One morning a group of elders from the villages slowly approached, looking very grim and angry. They were accompanied by a young woman who was visibly pregnant. Arrisa was her name. Arrisa had always brought flowers to the hermitage, and her soft eyes, laughter and elegant demeanour gave a special grace to the gatherings there. With downcast eyes and hesitant speech Arrisa stated publicly, in front of the elders, that the Rishi was the father of her unborn child.

The Rishi paused in what he was doing and looked at Arrisa with deep compassion and love in his eyes. He was silent for a while, then simply said "Very well." The elders left one by one, feeling deeply betrayed in the trust they had placed in the Rishi, and they and their villagers did not return.

Arrisa stayed at the hermitage in a separate room, and not once did the Rishi rebuke her for her falsehood. She took upon herself household and garden responsibilities. At the time of her confinement, several women from her village came to assist with the birth. They saw the separate living arrangements, but brought neither offerings, nor respect to the Rishi. To all this the Rishi simply said, "Very well."

A healthy son was born to Arrisa, yet she was torn and tormented by what she had done. She took wonderful care of the hermitage, the farm animals and the garden, growing the most beautiful flowers ever seen in that region.

She saw how the Rishi continued with his daily prayers and meditations. He diligently and joyfully conducted the seasonal ceremonies just as before. No one was present except for Arrisa and her son, or so she thought. Then she noticed how the farm animals would come closer to the hermitage, and sit nearby when the Rishi gave his teachings. He spoke to everything, to the birds gathered in the trees, the insects rustling in the grass, the whisper of wind and to the animals gathered close to him. His heart was full, just as before, and he was happy to be with whatever was there.

Arrisa could stand it no longer. One morning she told the Rishi that she was taking her son to meet the village elders, and tell them that the father of the child was a young man in a neighbouring village. He had left the region to join the army and be posted to a far-away location. The Rishi looked at her with the same compassionate eyes and simply said, "Very well."

Afterwards the elders and villagers began to return to the hermitage, full of apologies for their judgements, and for abandoning the teachings, saying how much they had missed his guidance and kindness. To all this the Rishi merely smiled and simply said "Very well." Arrisa and her son continued living at the hermitage. The father of her child returned to the region and married her. He asked the Rishi if he could stay at the hermitage with his new wife and child, and serve the Rishi as his attendant for the rest of his life. The Rishi looked at the young man with the same loving and compassionate eyes that he had presented to Arrisa. And we all know that he smiled and simply said, "Very well!"

His equanimity had revealed the truth of everything.

Equanimity is the fourth aspect of True Love in the Buddha's teachings. The other components are Loving Kindness, Compassion and Joy and they all grow from the ground provided by Equanimity.

26. Return to the Cave

January 26, 2008, was the peak of my training in Remembering, the letting go of resistance to all that Trailing Sky meant to me. She was an 18th century medicine woman from the American southwest who sought my attention in the 21st century.

Shera, a trusted and gifted astrologer friend, had repeatedly insisted that this date was mega significant for me and I had noted the day in my diary with a large underlined asterisk. It completed a two hundred and thirty one year cycle stretching back in time from January 26, 2008 to 1777, where I died in a prior life cradled in the arms of Trailing Sky Six Feathers. She vowed to find me in a future time to complete my purpose.

Needless to say there was insurmountable resistance from my intellectual and logical mind to remember that pledge in present time. I was clumsy about what was being woven. She initiated a dream vision on January 26, 2008 that culminated my slow process of remembering a clear mosaic of experiences stretching back in time over this rare cycle of two hundred and thirty-one years.

I had a healthy skepticism about astrology, yet learned how brilliant a scientist Shera was, with a mystic's gift of startling insight. Her accuracy was uncanny, detailed and constantly surprising. Her science was rigorous as she used the ancient texts for me, in addition to standard reference material. What struck Shera very forcibly as she researched my intersecting charts was Pluto peaking in Capricorn in every one of my 2008 astrological charts. She also noted, with some relief, that this signified the end of struggle for me. The internal battles were done, karma reversed, so I could look forward to ease and alignment. This date of January 26, 2008 was the major watershed of my lives.

It so happened that in the week leading up to January 26, 2008 I was at Fish Lake on the west side of Orlando, Florida. I stayed with friends who had a beautiful home on the shoreline of this conservation lake at the end of the Butler Lake chain. They invited me to their home each year to offer teachings to the Buddhist community in Orlando. Neither they nor I had any inkling of how significant this particular visit would be for me. There were few houses on the lake and so many wonderful creatures. All I needed was a pair of binoculars and a mug of coffee on their deck for paradise to unfold. The delight of seeing so many animals, birds, otters, possums and the occasional alligator was almost unspeakable.

With the approach of January 26th looming up in my diary I had decided to prepare by fasting and meditating deeply. There was actually no choice. I came down with stomach flu. Nothing that went into my mouth would stay down. Whatever bug had railroaded me, I actually welcomed the fast. That was definitely on, accompanied by a gentle entry into prolonged meditation that took me into deep humility to be in such a rare cradle of nature. But I was not tuning in at all to this two hundred and thirty-one year cycle that my astrology friend had been so emphatic about. No radical insights emerged, just jumbled rubbish dreams. Perhaps a clearing of my junk was taking place due to Pluto crashing into Capricorn with its usual uprooting panache.

The only thing I noticed on the evening before January 26 was that my focus suddenly became enlarged, as though my mind had moved from a small TV screen to a huge HD model. Perhaps a heightened lucidity that I attributed to being ill and light headed from the fasting.

During the night I had a vivid dream vision and remembered every exact detail. It was accompanied by a narrator speaking to me, which I found very odd:

I was standing on the lip of a cave high in a canyon in the Red Rock country of Central Arizona. An eagle flew up to me and alighted on my back. She wrapped her wings around me. The gentleness of the talons on my back and the embracing wings across my chest showed me that it was a female golden eagle. Her head was above mine, looking out from the cave. I could see through her eyes.

Then a narrator's voice said, "This is the protection of the great eagle. Trailing Sky Six Feathers gives it to you."

Then the mountain lion bounded into the cave and I heard a different voice in the dream, Trailing Sky speaking through the eagle. "This is the heart and courage of the mountain lion that I now give to you."

The deer came in, followed by owl and bear, all medicine gifts from Trailing Sky. The wily coyote trotted in, the gift of strategy and discernment.

The narrator spoke again, "This goes on throughout the night as you sleep. The gifts of Trailing Sky Six Feathers are given to you. Remember well, she is the greatest medicine woman the South West has ever known. Remember well, she is the direct expression of the highest universal plane. She had only one wish when you died in her arms two hundred and thirty-one years ago and that was to find you. Receive the gifts she could not give to you before you died. They arose in her to fill the void of your passing from her life. She has been waiting a long time. You promised her the last time you were in the cave sanctuary that you would understand and not resist."

"You now carry Trailing Sky's medicine bundle. Your illness was sent by her, so you would prepare without resistance. She connects to holy beings in all traditions. Guidance from her is not trivial and cannot ever be taken lightly. Your responsibility is to honor this. Your insights into the reality of Trailing Sky will become clear."

When I awoke next morning, I recalled the dream vision in precise detail. Suddenly I had a searing vision of Trailing Sky holding me in her arms as I died in 1777 at the medicine wheel on the rock bluff above a weeping willow tree. I was harrowed to the bone by her grief.

I felt her fierceness and anger at the other-worldly beings for failing to revive me. Then felt her anger release as she concentrated on my passage through time and space. I saw how she sat in the medicine wheel holding my dead body as she chanted our journey. I watched her hair turn grey, then white. Then saw her majestic communication to The People. I remember before death, looking up at her and smiling my love through my eyes to her and can still hear her say, "I will find you my husband. I will find you."

And she did, two hundred and thirty-one years later. I could not at first believe this or fully accept it. Yet the eagle wings around me were her arms, the eagle head above mine her vision and fierceness, the talons digging gently into my back to ensure that I understood.

In that instant I totally surrendered to this relentless Muse that never gave up on me. I gave up all resistance, realizing that Trailing Sky had kept her word from 1777, "*I will find you.*" Even now, as I write this memory down, I cannot stop the tears. I am both here, with the dream vision and there, dying in the medicine wheel, as she vows to find me. All my reservations and doubts become as nothing.

My life changed forever. That dream vision took me back to Trailing Sky's prophecy. I recalled to memory her last step across the lip of the cave when she stopped and went into a trance. I remember stepping closer to support her from falling. She had turned and spoke in a voice scarcely her own. "You will return to this cave in dreamtime, though not in this lifetime. Hear me now, understand the vision and do not resist what it teaches. Hear me and promise me."

She had offered her medicine gifts. I had finally "Remembered." So much from that time was flooding my mind. I knew that the medicine gifts received from Trailing Sky during the dream vision required that I nurture the skills within me to use them wisely.

I entered deeply into silence, meditation and reflection about the dream vision, keeping this all to myself. From my training in different wisdom traditions, I brought together the power inherent in them into the mental medicine wheel taught to me by White Eagle Woman. This was the altar, the preparation to honor this great being Trailing Sky Six Feathers.

In the centre of the medicine wheel mandala our daily conversations began. I had to take time and care to place the gifts from Trailing Sky in appropriate vessels for understanding and communication to others. My remaining time at Fish Lake, surrounded by nature and solitude, provided the uninterrupted space to allow this to deepen, so I could fully integrate the portent of the dream vision. I was very quiet, living simply in a disciplined and light manner, cultivating the vessels.

I also had some unexpected help. A magnificent osprey had roosted at the top of the dead tree in front of my bedroom window. He was there every sunrise during this time of fasting and insight. I would go out to the balcony on waking up and he would be right there. Not fishing. Not flying. Just there, staring in my direction. He would stay until noon.

On a hunch on the third morning, I walked over to the tall dead tree and found several feathers. On the fourth morning, right after the dream vision, I stepped out on to the balcony and there he was again. He stretched his wings, preened his feathers and let out a high-pitched squawk. I mused, "I guess you are there to make sure I got it about the dream vision and Trailing Sky's prophecy."

Whether he picked my thoughts out of the sky I will never know, but with a resounding high pitched screech he spread his wings and flew in a huge circle over Fish Lake and then headed west up the chain of lakes. I got dressed and headed over to the tree where he had perched. There were more feathers. I picked them up and added the feathers to my collection. I had not counted them, but when I did there were exactly six feathers. I started to laugh as tears of joy and understanding ran down my face. I got the message, and chuckled at the osprey who could count.

I was in awe of the dream vision, the medicine gifts, and the narrator. The implications for my life were enormous. All my reservations and doubts were as nothing compared to the gifts bestowed upon me by Trailing Sky Six Feathers. I did not take the six feathers home with me. They were a communication, not a keepsake. I enjoyed a quiet paddle through the lake system and buried the six feathers, bound by grass, at the foot of a tree containing a huge osprey nest.

This was my gratitude.

Four Phases / Dr. Ian Prattis

PHASE FOUR: CARING FOR THE PLANET

Four Phases / Dr. Ian Prattis

27.   Weaving Autumn in the Canyon

Silver birches silhouette the sky,
gather in numbers,
silently,
elegantly, grace "en pointe."

Sway and breathe
bend and whisper in the canyon,
leaves shimmer
dancing to gathering wind.

Murmur Creation's tones
in synchrony with stellar rhythms,
their sound carries waves
rolling into shoreline rocks.
Silver birches silhouette the sky.

Light of Sun climbs the sacred canyon
rushing down islands
while shaping Life's meanings.
Sunset fills the sky,
tracing Creator's name
to the rim of eternity.
Right now to every heart,
clouds muster and shadow a
gentle cascade of evening.

This symphony of autumn color,
melody from a sky
pastel grey and fiery red.
Descant to the tones
of a painted forest
cooled by lush evergreens.

Sensual beauty,
rhapsody of forest, canyon and sunset
fused as a golden sheen.

All caught in a still lake
waiting with patience,
beyond time and space
to reflect this moment of splendor.

Weaving.

28.   Dance of the Eyes

Enter the Muse – waiting
for cracks in façade's crumble.
Grant life to dancing with the eyes

Soft spoken adoration blows on dandelions,
parasols drifting to fertile ground.
Awakening pirouette turning en pointe,
while the waltz of happiness
leaves all sadness behind.

A funeral march to banish pain elsewhere,
before our eyes danced together.
Life lives in each glance,
cradled in the mosaic of
connecting where the universe begins and ends.

Delicate curves of elegant quadrilles
with the peace of loving serenade.
We dance with our eyes,
intensity of convulsive samba, cheek to cheek.

All in place, this dance of our eyes.

29. The Old Oak Tree

The gnarled old Oak tree
garnished by its leaves
lit up with daily sunrise.
Encourage children to climb
and seek far away fields
in the distance from
this tree with billowing sails.

The waving boughs of the old Oak
set a course for ocean adventures
until evening darkens.
Kids wait for the rising
of the next day,
where travelling to new vistas
emerge on the old tree.

The old Oak Tree
provides shade for shy deer
even the rare sight of coyote –
or was it a fox, maybe a bear
shouted one child to another.
Held beautifully by the garnished
leaves and sturdy branches,
shimmering for animals and children.

The gnarled old Oak Tree
sighed in satisfaction.

30.   Creation Calling

Resonance through time
unfolds the origin of Creation.
Stretching the songs of love
for the Universe to escape
and be different
to what it was.
Expanding this wish to the hearts
of oceans, trees, creatures and humans.

The drum of the Universe
clasped on my arm,
attuned to tectonic depths with ease.

I rest and learn
through skin, muscle, bone, guts
and the smallest atom -
that stark light drives the Universe.
It begins with the smallest molecule
edging to Creation's direction,
through spectrums circling.

Compassion, clarity, seeking truth -
bring life into splendour from darkness.
The Creation of the universe knows
authentic beings
without being a self.

Every molecule engages the Universal threads
in the warp of ruthless identity.
Floating free to the
largest constellation,
authentic rests
without ego, self or impression.
It infuses Love, Peace Integrity.

Being is enough.
Casting realms of delight
to the passion of being.
Realms carried higher
from dust sprinkled
through every warp.

That is where we belong.

31.   Ancient Tree in Winter

Ancient Tree in Winter,
where did you come from?
Now trapped,
cleft by rocks at river's edge.
Water eddies carve your shape.

Ice mires your branches,
snow creeps fingers across the river
as your body disappears under deep snow.
Decaying sculpture of existence.

Death and birth are here
as your journey carries you through.
Ducks stand on broken limbs
while preening their feathers.

Did you once stand tall and majestic
in a gentle Rideau River valley?
Host to birds, small animals,
insects and whispering breeze?

Were you alone on a high bluff,
shading thundering rapids
that pulled you to their embrace?

What felled you
so that you now lie here
trapped cleft by rocks?
Exquisite beauty of my winter river walk
just wait for spring's flood to set you free.

32. The River Speaks

Sunlight through trees
dance on last year's leaves
by river's edge.

Voices carry the struggle upstream
against the current, into the wind.
The mighty river spoke to russet forests,
female sources creating intergenerational wisdom
that we hardly touch and rarely heed.

You are here Ancient Wisdom,
shimmering through the river's embrace.
Pacing rapids, knee deep in the river's grip,
the raging water threatens
our yellow canoe.
Asserting dominion,
is the way running through Mother Earth.
Weakened by portages,
cut and scratched by thorns, burnt by sun.
Shoulders aching, back burning
from the ascent of rapids,
searching deep for strength.

Then the wondrous peace of waiting in silence
by river's edge.
Taking the moment to flow
with this river as she speaks quietly
to yellow canoe.

Of wavelets losing themselves
dying on a gently shelving beach.

Each day, before the elements reveal their majesty,
a gift from nature
is brought by the wind
crashing into our senses.
We recognize storm, snow, wind and torrents,
gifts to our opening experience to wonder.

Snow dusts our tents
white upon orange,
reflecting the fire's dying embers
glowing charcoal red.
Placed on a point in Quebec
we listen to the rattle of box cars
behind the CN train,
snaking past on the south shore
travelling west more quickly.

Slowly the camp returns to nature.
All traces removed of our presence
except our memories,
for whoever else finds this spot of glory.
Frozen socks, scarves, underwear
left overnight on cedar branches
crackle and bend
as they are folded, stiff into ice-rimmed packs.

We run against rapids
where ospreys have their nest.
Wheeling in the sky,

gazing down at our struggle
to mount minor rapids.
"Going the wrong way!" the ospreys scream.
They are masters of their domain
only we are not of ours.

Listen —
listen to the sound of it.
To the feel of it
raining gently down,
separating each droplet of rain
as it enters the womb of earth
through the river.

Then we are gone
replacing the camp
with our absence.

Presence remains
in individual gratitude
for the intergenerational threads
we are thankful for.
I take from this place
a white blossom overhanging
the riverbank,
and adorn the yellow canoe
with nature's bounty.

An indigenous friend – Mohawk -
with the name of a familiar,
Bear.
Came to our solitude

by this mist laden river
He found us quietly connecting to the past,
with magnificence around and within us.
Bear politely took us from this place
to a bridge close by.

His flat board truck waiting
to take us to Fort William,
locale of the Hudson Bay Company's past splendor.
A trading post from another era,
once a drawing point for trappers,
hunters, voyageurs, first nations, traders
and river lovers.

All came here for weddings,
furs, funerals and ceremonial feasts.
We stayed this night at the fur trading post.
surrounded by a stand of
red and white pine
tall and majestic.
Nurtured not logged.

I repeopled with all that was past
—feeling the future's strands unfold as they must.

33. Childhood Bedrooms

Andrei asked her a surprising question, "When you were a child what was your bedroom like?"

Katerina smiled as fond recollections arose in her mind. "I had the most marvelous bedroom. It was more of a music room than a bedroom, full of musical instruments."

She then laughed, "I had all these stuffed animals and would place them next to instruments and move them around. My father was such a lovely goof. He would knock on the door and ask if he was to be Elephant, Tinker Bell or Bear and then come in and play their instruments."

Andrei was rolling over with laughter, as she continued. "My bedroom had a large bay window and my father would sit there with whatever stuffed animal I assigned to him. Often my mother would come in and conduct the entire ensemble."

Katerina's face was lit up with the memories and she turned to him, "What about you Andrei?"

He pondered whether to reveal too much, then decided to do so. "My bedroom as a child was my sanctuary. My parents were often under police scrutiny due to their beliefs. To compensate they created a very safe haven for me."

He slowly gathered himself, "In one corner I remember books, paintings and wooden stools piled in disarray. My bed had two levels, one for me to sleep upon and the other for my stuffed animals to talk to before sleeping. It was a comfortable bed with large pillows and green checkered blankets. I had a telescope next to the window and I would fly to galaxies with my favorite animals."

Then he paused, "Perhaps it was too much of a sanctuary, as I did not like to leave this house. I had to when my parents entered the Space Agency in Moscow. I did not want to leave my safe bedroom behind but my father was very smart. He cleared it out and painted it in colors I hated. I begged him and my mother to let me see it one last time."

There was a tremor of emotion in Andrei's voice and Katerina stayed very still. "On that last visit, mother pointed to the empty window where my telescope once focused on the sky. I felt the loss, stripped down in an empty space once resonant with discovery. I felt my mother's gentle hands on my shoulder and still remember

her saying, 'There is nothing to hold you back, Andrei. Your dream is still inside. Now you can step into freedom."

He continued, "Mother smiled as I looked for the telescope. Nothing was there. My treasures were boxed and sent on to Moscow."

Andrei then said, "This was their way to move me on from fear rather than cling to childhood safety. My mother held my hand and I stared at the spot where the telescope was no longer there."

Katerina reached over and gently closed her hands around his, "And here you are Andrei. I will hold you steady. For always."

He looked at her and raised her hand to his lips and gently kissed her fingers.

34. A Healing Journey

See yourself walking through a beautiful meadow, full of flowers. You hear the sounds of insects humming and birds singing. The sun feels warm on your face and a slight breeze ruffles your hair. As you walk look up into an endlessly clear blue sky and for a moment allow yourself to merge with it and enter such clarity.

(Pause – breathing IN and OUT for two minutes)

Notice a small shape hovering in the sky that gets bigger as it comes closer to you. It is a golden eagle slowly circling above you. He is your guardian and will watch over you and keep you safe on your journey. The meadow slowly gives way to a river that runs over rocks before eddying into deep, still pools. Follow the bank of the river in the direction of the sun. There is a path to walk along. Notice the mallard ducks at the water's edge with their ducklings, and a kingfisher sitting patiently on a branch overhanging a deep, still pool. The sun filters through the trees at the river's edge and the light dances on the rocks and water like a crystal cloak that shimmers and moves with every swirl and eddy.

(Pause – breathing IN and OUT for two minutes)

Walking around a bend, you see that the river runs into a clear lake fringed with forests, reflecting snow-capped mountains in its still surface. Find your place by the side of the lake, sit down and enjoy the intimacy of nature that is around you. At the end of the lake you see a cow moose with her calf at the water's edge. In the distance you hear wolves calling to one another and notice two rabbits beside a shrub close by. A doe and two fawns walk slowly and tentatively from the forest into the sunlight. Skylarks hover motionless in the sky then descend to earth with their lilting song. Your eyes are drawn to a stately blue heron standing motionless in the reeds at the lake's edge. These creatures are there to remind you of your connection to the world of nature. Take a moment to be with the grass, the trees, animals, birds, insects, and bring your favourite animals.

(Pause – breathing IN and OUT for two minutes)

Ask one of the creatures to accompany you on your journey and wait to see which one comes forward. It does not matter if none come forward, the golden eagle still circles overhead as your guardian.

(Pause – breathing IN and OUT for two minutes)

After sitting by the lake's edge for a while, stand up and slowly walk into the water. It is icy cold, fed by glaciers from the snow-capped mountains. But it is a cold that is bearable because it purifies, stripping you of your anxieties, stress and worries. Slowly walk into the water up to your hips, your chest and then submerge yourself in the icy cold embrace of purification. Underwater, you can breathe and move around with ease. Notice the rays of sunlight entering the water, fish swimming swiftly past and see the rocks and submerged tree trunks on the lake floor. As you move around and adjust to the water you see a cave at the bottom of the lake and you swim strongly and powerfully to enter it. There is light at the end of a long underwater passage and you swim through and emerge out of the water into a cavern covered in crystals. The sound from the crystals shimmers through your body. At the edge of the cavern is a waterfall. Stand underneath it and feel the water washing over and right through your body. Feel the energy of the waterfall taking away your anxiety, tension and distress.

(Pause – breathing IN and OUT for two minutes)

Leave the cavern and follow a trail that takes you through a pine forest. Beautiful tall pines are on either side of you, stretching up into the sky. Take a moment and see the entire blue sky endlessly clear and enter such clarity.

(Pause – breathing IN and OUT for two minutes)

Then see how the forest opens up into a large clearing with a big flat rock in the center. There is a fire prepared for you by the rock. As you warm your hands by the fire and feel its warmth on your face, there is a presence next to you. Turning around, you see a beautiful old woman with clear brown eyes that look right into you. She smiles in welcome and you feel she knows all about you and embraces you in a simple, heartfelt love. She is a very powerful healer, a wise shaman and is there on your journey to serve you.

(Pause – breathing IN and OUT for two minutes)

Standing next to her is a handsome old man, with weathered features and a gentle smile that lights you up. From his eyes, you feel overwhelming compassion and understanding. He is a very powerful healer and a wise shaman and is there on your journey to serve you.

(Pause – breathing IN and OUT for two minutes)

Between the old man and old woman is a young woman who sparkles. She is fresh, vibrant and beautiful, aglow with life's vitality. She also greets you with a smile and a love that you know is unconditional. She is the feminine source of Earth Wisdom and a lightning rod for your transformation. She knows very well the suffering and chaos of modern times. She is a very powerful healer and a wise shaman and is there on your journey to serve you. Particularly if you are at the crossroads of New Beginnings and ready to discard the old damaging tapes you run in your mind. Her power has an infinite depth and force.

(Pause – breathing IN and OUT for two minutes)

Know that these three shamans also come from the deepest part of your mind and they represent your own powers of creativity and self-healing. The three shamans approach you and invite you to speak to them. Choose who you wish to communicate with, then talk about whatever distresses you: the anxieties of the day, the stresses at work and at home, then if you wish, go deeper into your distress. Talk to them about growing up, the neglect and abuse you may have experienced, the isolation, separation and lack of understanding you encountered as a young person, adolescent and adult. Talk about the damage caused to you and the damage you have caused to others. Talk about the hatreds, angers and insensitivities you experience and perpetuate. You can say anything to these three shamans. They understand and love you and are there to heal you. Talk about whatever you feel free to communicate and feel the distress and trauma leaving your body. And when you run out of things to say, just be with their loving and supportive presence. For now, open up and speak to one of these immensely powerful shamans placed on your path.

(Long Pause – Breathing IN and OUT for five minutes)

Ask each one of them if they would transfer their power of creativity, understanding and healing to your awareness. Of course they will agree. Look into the eyes of each one of them in turn and feel the transfer of their healing power with a jolt or energy circulation within your body. Thank them for this gift, then ask if you could speak to someone from the other side. Someone who has passed on, that you did not have the opportunity to share what you wanted to say, or hear what you would have liked to hear. Wait and see if anyone comes and do not be disappointed if nothing happens. It is not the time.

(Pause – breathing IN and OUT for two minutes)

Take your leave of the shamans. Thank them for their support, love and power of healing. Turning around, you see a beautiful child surrounded with a golden aura. This golden child is you, without trauma, wounds or damage. The child comes directly to you and takes your hand, and leads you to a cliff edge where the beautiful golden eagle is waiting for you. He has been there as a guardian throughout your journey and is now ready to take you home.

(Pause – breathing IN and OUT for two minutes)

Ask your golden child if he or she wants to come with you, then climb onto the back of the eagle, and feel him take off from the ledge and soar high on the updrafts. Below you, see the mountains, lakes and forests of your journey. Smoke curls lazily skyward from the fire by the rock and as you fly with the eagle feel how beautiful this earth is. Then when you feel ready, leave the eagle and fly on your own with your golden child next to you. With your arms spread wide as wings, catch the air currents and soar, then swoop low over the streams and mountains and enjoy the strength of flying on your own as your golden child merges with you, creating one unified being.

(Pause – breathing IN and OUT for two minutes)

Slowly fly back to the edge of the lake where you were sitting. Once again notice the animals, birds and insects and see how happy they are to see you again. Sit there for a time.

(Pause – breathing IN and OUT for two minutes)

See yourself lying down in a healing circle. Form a circle of brilliant white light around where you are lying down, then step through the light and slowly return to your body. Breathe deeply on the in-breath and exhale deeply on the out-breath. As you breathe in, say quietly to yourself, "I have arrived". As you breathe out, say quietly to yourself, "I am home". Continue this breathing exercise for at least five minutes or until you feel "arrived" and "home" in your body.

35. Taking Refuge in Grandchildren

Taking refuge can provide surprises. It is not always a dharma teacher, wise sister or high monk who is there to provide solace and guidance. My grandson Callun has provided quite a few surprises for me.

Callun's home is on Vancouver Island in British Columbia. One summer holiday Carolyn and I spent a sea kayaking adventure with Callun and his father Iain, exploring the fascinating coastline of Vancouver Island.

On one occasion when Iain and Carolyn went shopping, I stayed at the house to meditate. Callun was playing outside. He came in crying after a while and tapped me on the shoulder. "Grand Pooh Bear" – that is what he called me when he was a little boy – "Grand Pooh Bear, sorry to disturb your practice but I've been stung by a bee on my neck and it hurts."

I opened my eyes and took Callun into my arms and said: "My dear Callun, you *are* my practice."

I gently took the stinger out of his neck, put some ice on it and cuddled him for a while before he happily went outside again to play. He had brought home to me that all of life is my practice. To my grandson Callun I bow down in gratitude for being such a mindfulness bell for me.

When I take refuge in this manner, I am aware of Buddha nature being graciously presented to me.

I recall another grandchild, Millie, sending me some drawings for my birthday many years ago. With her five year old determination she drew a picture of me – no feet, only one arm, with a fuzzy beard, jug handle ears and much slimmer than in reality! Over my head she'd drawn a yellow halo, which is totally undeserving, yet I learned from her mother that this was how Millie thought of me. Millie was revealing her Buddha nature to her grandfather and I joyfully took refuge in her love and kindness.

Several years ago, after leading a meditation retreat on the British Columbia mainland I arranged to take a ferry across to Nanaimo on Vancouver Island to visit with my son and grandson Callun. It was a beautiful calm sea voyage with the sunset dancing in the ferry's wake. Though I was tired from the retreat, this was a delightful respite.

Both Iain and Callun were there as the boat docked in Nanaimo. As it was almost Callun's bedtime, he asked if I would read him a story once we got to their home. I was happy to do this. Callun quickly changed into his pyjamas and chose a story for me to read. I lay down on his bed beside him and started to read. In only a few minutes I was fast asleep! My son, Iain, on hearing the silence, came into the bedroom and saw that Callun had pulled the bedcovers up over me and was sitting up in bed with one hand resting lightly on my shoulder, a beautiful smile on his face as he took care of his grandfather. My son was moved to tears by this. He drew a chair into the bedroom and sat there with us for several hours. He did not want to miss the magic.

Three generations taking refuge in one another. Totally present, hearts wide open. Only one snoring, but gently!

36.   COVID–19 and Walking Meditation

Anxiety and fear fuel the internal stress about the Coronavirus driven by the global pandemic. Masks, distancing and small gatherings are necessary while COVID–19 overwhelms practices that create and maintain healthy mental health.

Our modern society faces collective disruption and the uncertainty of polarization while the COVID–19 virus and variants continue to mutate. It does not discriminate, so no-one is safe.

Until such time as populations are fully vaccinated, this virus will continue to spread a variety of deadly variants. I have lost several friends and colleagues who died from COVID–19. They did not have vaccines.

The pandemic is global and at the present time multiple vaccines are required. COVID–19 has plunged our world into drastic deaths. It requires our diligence to take vaccines, keep distance and wear masks. The poorer countries in the world are without such measures and plunge into a desperate break-down into death. COVID-19 and its various variants require global medicine measures to cure the pandemic. It is not really a matter of choice - it is a societal measure. Failure to vaccinate puts others at risk.

Simply examine the deaths and cases in Canada over the past months and notice the number of victims without vaccines. Spiritual beings, holistic and natural healers are not immune, though many think they are. In fact, COVID–19 overwhelms them.

It is often impossible to calm and meditate during such a pandemic but we can, however, learn to walk with normal breaths for 15 minutes – in our home, in our back yard or around our streets – making sure we honor distance from others.

We know from our experience of hikes in nature, or neighborhood walks after dinner, that sudden flashes of insight often arise in concert with our footsteps. We can see clearly how to handle the predicament of COVID–19.

Imagine what can happen when we add conscious awareness to our footsteps. When we concentrate on our breath and focus on slow walking, we actually have a brilliant piece of engineering to quiet the mind and body.

When we add a third concentration – aware of how our feet touch the earth – we have a meditative practice designed for our difficult times. We focus our mind on the mechanism of each foot touching the earth – heel, then ball of foot, then toe. We slow down even further and with our body – not our intellect or ego – we make a contract with Mother Earth to leave a smaller footprint. We examine our consumption patterns, COVID–19, energy use and the impact of Climate Change - all from walking with awareness, our breath, our legs and noticing how our feet touch the earth.

With this concentrated focus of walking meditation there is very little opportunity for the mind to worry about past events or future anticipations.

The meditation keeps us present, here in the moment of being fully alive. It slows us down step by step so that our mind enters silence. This is aided by another component we can add to walking meditation – a gentle half smile to nurture the peace and silence within.

With the deepening of this internal silence, insight naturally occurs.

Walking meditation is a powerful methodology for healing and mental health. We start by breathing in and out with full attention to the in-breath and to the out-breath.

Co-ordinating our breath with our steps we breathe in, saying silently to ourselves – "Breathing in" - as we take two or three slow steps. Then as we breathe out, we say – "Breathing out" – as we simultaneously take two or three slow steps. Practice this for several minutes just to get used to the concentration and co-ordination of breath and steps.

Be fully aware of breathing in and out, and of walking slowly step by step.

Allow the breath and lungs to find a natural rhythm with your steps. It is the concentration and awareness that matters, not whether you take two or three steps, but do remember to wear a half smile on your lips!

As you take each step, you can add a concentration that brings you solidly into contact with Mother Earth. Concentrate on your foot touching the ground in this sequence – heel, ball of foot, toe. This particular concentration assists you to be fully with your stepping on the earth, keeping you alert to earth rhythms.

At Carleton University in Ottawa where I was a professor, I would walk from the bus stop and take a detour around the greenhouses of the Botany department and come to the Rideau River that runs along one side of the campus.

From there I had a kilometre of riverbank to practice walking meditation before arriving at my office building. It is quite secluded in parts and the river has sets of rapids that greatly enrich my walk.

One section of the path takes my steps through a cedar grove, and I always felt a sacred blessing from these beautiful trees. I slow my walking right down to a three–three rhythm when I enter the cedar grove. The path is never the same, as the seasons change their character. Autumn leaves give way to snowfall as winter leaves her embrace.

My clothes and footwear change, yet my steps, breathing and feet touching the earth remain constant. The rustle of autumn leaves is replaced by the crunch of snow and ice, which gives way to the mud and rain of spring before the heat of summer allows me to walk in sandals or barefoot.

The birds and foliage change with the seasons, as does the river – iced over in winter, turbulent in the spring and calm in summer and fall. Students with their books and friends congregate by the river when the weather is sunny.

I notice the changes in the seasonal round of nature, yet remain with my breathing, footsteps and the earth – so that I am not drawn into unnecessary thought.

It takes me approximately twenty minutes to arrive at my office. I am in a clear, calm state and better able to be of assistance to students and colleagues and bring my own sense of calm and clarity to the university.

On leaving the university I retrace my steps of walking meditation along the river before going home, or to appointments in the city. The experience engenders the same calm and clarity.

This walk is paradise and a constant reminder to me for those occasions when I am not in touch with the Earth Mother. We do not need to walk on water, or over hot coals.

We simply need to walk on the earth and touch her deeply with our full awareness. That is all that walking meditation is.

Four Phases / Dr. Ian Prattis

ABOUT THE AUTHOR

At a writer's retreat, the facilitator who had read my book **Redemption** spoke of it as if she were listening to music. The cadence of my writing struck her forcibly. I often described **Redemption** as an extended prose poem, but liked her musical note metaphor much more. I then learned **Trailing Sky Six Feathers** had received the Quill Award from Focus on Women Magazine, an advocacy group for women's issues worldwide. I was delighted that this award came from a women's group. Other awards include Gold for **Redemption** at the 2015 Florida Book Festival, Silver for Environment from the 2014 Living Now Literary Awards for **Failsafe; Saving the Earth From Ourselves.** There was the 2019 Gold for **Our World Is Burning** from the eLit Excellence Awards, followed by the 2021 Silver medal for **Past, Present, Future; Stories that Haunt.** My book **Shattered Earth** also received the 2020 Gold Medal from the eLit Excellence Awards. I received the 2011 Ottawa Earth Day Environment Award and the 2018 Yellow Lotus award from the Vesak Project for spiritual guidance and teaching dharma.

FOUR PHASES: Lost, Impermanence, Bittersweet, Caring is my 19th book, perhaps the most difficult yet. It is about our broken world and Climate Emergency. My books are not candidates for intellectual sophistry or for theological nicety. Such signposts should not be held onto. It is the reader's inner experience of the words that is worthwhile. If the reader clings to a formula with the mistaken belief that it holds the truth, then one must be prepared for disappointment. Formulas for truth expand into rigidly held beliefs, that deny reality. This leads to an escape that is strategic, an escape from knowing and experiencing the energy of inner consciousness. When these dependencies are abandoned through trust in one's inner journey, celebrate what has always resided within. This is what I hope the reader will reconcile with a viable strategy for our times, so readers, citizens and leaders are equipped with tools that generate understanding, compassion and non-violent reconciliation.

Our experience of inner truth, of true nature, the warp and weft of the universal tapestry, the seeing of sound in falling snowflakes, the texture of wind in leaves at moonlight, the symphony of song is there in a mountain stream. All that's required is that you show up for life in each moment and be a spiritual warrior. My writing is that of a Poet, life as a Global Traveler, Founder of Friends for Peace, Guru in India, Zen teacher - enables the spiritual warrior within to focus on planetary care, peace and social justice.

I presently live in Ottawa, Canada and encourage people to find their true nature, so that humanity and the planet may be renewed. I mostly stay local to help turn the tide in my home city so that good things begin to happen spontaneously. My poetry, memoirs, fiction, articles, blogs and podcasts appear in a wide range of venues. Beneath the polished urban facade remains a part of human nature that few acknowledge, because it is easier to deny the basic instincts that have kept us alive on an unforgiving earth.

I bravely go into literary work. A stone tossed into the oceans of life.

PUBLICATIONS – THE AUTHOR'S WORKS

- New Directions in Economic Anthropology: Canadian Review of Sociology and Anthropology, 1973

- Reflections: The Anthropological Muse: American Anthropological Association, 1985

- Leadership and Ethics: RSVK, May 1997

- Anthropology at the Edge: Essays on Culture, Symbol and Consciousness: University Press of America, 1997

- The Essential Spiral: Ecology and Consciousness After 9/11: University Press of America, 2002

- Failsafe: Saving The Earth From Ourselves: Manor House Publishing, 2011

- Earth My Body, Water My Blood: Baico Publishing Inc. 2011

- Song of Silence: Baico Publishing Inc. 2011

- Portals and Passages. Book 1 and Book 2, Amazon Kindle. 2012

- Keeping Dharma Alive. Volume 1 & Volume 2, Amazon Kindle, 2012

- Redemption, Xlibris LLC, 2014

- Trailing Sky Six Feathers: One Man's Journey with His Muse, Xlibris LLC, 2014

- New Planet New World, Manor House Publishing, 2016

- Our World is Burning; My Views on Mindful Engagement, Manor House Publishing, 2017

- Painting with Words; Poetry for a New Era, Manor House Publishing, 2018

- Shattered Earth: Approaching Extinction, Manor House Publishing, 2021

- Past, Present, Future: Stories that Haunt, Manor House Publishing, 2021

- 2 CD's and 3 DVD's; 4 films

- 10 Professional Honors

- 36 Television Classes at Carleton University and on Ontario TVO

- 50 articles in Pine Gate – Online Buddhist Journal; 250 articles in newspapers, community magazines, 200 professional articles/chapters/book reviews

Manor House / 905-648-4797
www.manor-house-publishing.com

Manor House / 905-648-4797
www.manor-house-publishing.com